ENCYCLICAL LETTER
CENTESIMUS ANNUS
OF THE SUPREME PONTIFF

JOHN PAUL II

ON THE
HUNDREDTH ANNIVERSARY
OF *RERUM NOVARUM*

St. Paul Books & Media

Vatican Translation
Editing (inclusive language) Daughters of St. Paul

ISBN 0-8198-5418-2

Printed and published in the U.S.A., by St. Paul Books & Media
50 St. Paul's Avenue, Boston, MA 02130

St. Paul Books & Media is the publishing house of the Daughters of
St. Paul, an international congregation of women religious serving the
Church with the communications media.

2 3 4 5 6 7 8 9   98 97 96 95 94 93 92 91

Contents

Contents

Venerable Brothers,
Beloved Sons and Daughters,
Health and the Apostolic Blessing!

Introduction

1. The Centenary of the promulgation of the encyclical which begins with the words *"Rerum Novarum,"*[1] by my predecessor of venerable memory Pope Leo XIII, is an occasion of great importance for the present history of the Church and for my own pontificate. It is an encyclical that has the distinction of having been commemorated by solemn papal documents from its fortieth anniversary to its ninetieth. It may be said that its path through history has been marked by other documents which paid tribute to it and applied it to the circumstances of the day.[2]

In doing likewise for the hundredth anniversary, in response to requests from many bishops, Church institutions, and study centers, as well as business leaders and workers, both individually and as members of associations, I wish first and foremost to satisfy the debt of gratitude which the whole Church owes to this great Pope and his "immortal document."[3] I also mean to show that *the vital energies* rising from that root have not been spent with the passing of the years, but rather *have increased even more*. This is evident from the various initiatives which have preceded, and which are to accompany and follow the celebration, initiatives promoted by episcopal conferences, by international agencies, universities and academic institutes, by professional associations and by other institutions and individuals in many parts of the world.

2. The present encyclical is part of these celebrations, which are meant to thank God — the origin of "every good endowment and every perfect gift" (Jas 1:17) — for having used a document

published a century ago by the See of Peter to achieve so much good and to radiate so much light in the Church and in the world. Although the commemoration at hand is meant to honor *Rerum Novarum,* it also honors those encyclicals and other documents of my predecessors which have helped to make Pope Leo's encyclical present and alive in history, thus constituting what would come to be called the Church's "social doctrine," "social teaching" or even "social magisterium."

The validity of this teaching has already been pointed out in two encyclicals published during my pontificate: *Laborem Exercens* on human work, and *Sollicitudo Rei Socialis* on current problems regarding the development of individuals and peoples.[4]

3. I now wish to propose a "rereading" of Pope Leo's encyclical by issuing an invitation to "look back" at the text itself in order to discover anew the richness of the fundamental principles which it formulated for dealing with the question of the condition of workers. But this is also an invitation to "look around" at the "new things" which surround us and in which we find ourselves caught up, very different from the "new things" which characterized the final decade of the last century. Finally, it is an invitation to "look to the future" at a time when we can already glimpse the third millennium of the Christian era, so filled with uncertainties but also with promises—uncertainties and promises which appeal to our imagination and creativity, and which reawaken our responsibility, as disciples of the "one teacher" (cf. Mt 23:8), to show the way, to proclaim the truth and to communicate the life which is Christ (cf. Jn 14:6).

A rereading of this kind will not only confirm *the permanent value of such teaching,* but will also manifest *the true meaning of the Church's Tradition* which, being ever living and vital, builds upon the foundation laid by our fathers in the faith, and particularly upon what "the Apostles passed down to the Church"[5] in the name of Jesus Christ, who is her irreplaceable foundation (cf. 1 Cor 3:11).

It was out of an awareness of his mission as the successor of Peter that Pope Leo XIII proposed to speak out, and Peter's successor today is moved by that same awareness. Like Pope Leo and the popes before and after him, I take my inspiration from the Gospel image of "the scribe who has been trained for the kingdom of heaven," whom the Lord compares to "a householder who brings out of his treasure what is new and what is old" (Mt 13:52). The treasure is the great outpouring of the Church's Tradition, which contains "what is old" — received and passed on from the very beginning — and which enables us to interpret the "new things" in the midst of which the life of the Church and the world unfolds.

Among the things which become "old" as a result of being incorporated into Tradition, and which offer opportunities and material for enriching both Tradition and the life of faith, there is the fruitful activity of many millions of people, who, spurred on by the social Magisterium, have sought to make that teaching the inspiration for their involvement in the world. Acting either as individuals or joined together in various groups, associations and organizations, these people represent a *great movement for the defense of the human person* and the safeguarding of human dignity. Amid changing historical circumstances, this movement has contributed to the building up of a more just society or at least to the curbing of injustice.

The present encyclical seeks to show the fruitfulness of the principles enunciated by Leo XIII, which belong to the Church's doctrinal patrimony and, as such, involve the exercise of her teaching authority. But pastoral solicitude also prompts me to propose *an analysis of some events of recent history.* It goes without saying that part of the responsibility of pastors is to give careful consideration to current events in order to discern the new requirements of evangelization. However, such an analysis is not meant to pass definitive judgments, since this does not fall *per se* within the Magisterium's specific domain.

Chapter I

Characteristics of *Rerum Novarum*

4. Towards the end of the last century the Church found herself facing an historical process which had already been taking place for some time, but which was by then reaching a critical point. The determining factor in this process was a combination of radical changes which had taken place in the political, economic and social fields, and in the areas of science and technology, to say nothing of the wide influence of the prevailing ideologies. In the sphere of politics, the result of these changes was a *new conception of society and of the State,* and consequently *of authority itself.* A traditional society was passing away and another was beginning to be formed — one which brought the hope of new freedoms but also the threat of new forms of injustice and servitude.

In the sphere of economics, in which scientific discoveries and their practical application come together, new structures for the production of consumer goods had progressively taken shape. A *new form of property* had appeared — capital; and a *new form of labor* — labor for wages, characterized by high rates of production which lacked due regard for sex, age or family situation, and were determined solely by efficiency, with a view to increasing profits.

In this way labor became a commodity to be freely bought and sold on the market, its price determined by the law of supply and demand, without taking into account the bare minimum required for the support of the individual and his family. Moreover, the worker was not even sure of being able to sell "his own commodity," continually threatened as he was by unemployment, which, in the absence of any kind of social security, meant the specter of death by starvation.

The result of this transformation was a society "divided into two classes, separated by a deep chasm."[6] This situation was linked to the marked change taking place in the political order already mentioned. Thus the prevailing political theory of the time sought to promote total economic freedom by appropriate laws, or, conversely, by a deliberate lack of any intervention. At the same time, another conception of property and economic life was beginning to appear in an organized and often violent form, one which implied a new political and social structure.

At the height of this clash, when people finally began to realize fully the very grave injustice of social realities in many places and the danger of a revolution fanned by ideals which were then called "socialist," Pope Leo XIII intervened with a document which dealt in a systematic way with the "condition of the workers." The encyclical had been preceded by others devoted to teachings of a political character; still others would appear later.[7] Here, particular mention must be made of the encyclical *Libertas Praestantissimum,* which called attention to the essential bond between human freedom and truth, so that freedom which refused to be bound to the truth would fall into arbitrariness and end up submitting itself to the vilest of passions, to the point of self-destruction. Indeed, what is the origin of all the evils to which *Rerum Novarum* wished to respond, if not a kind of freedom which, in the area of economic and social activity, cuts itself off from the truth about humanity?

The Pope also drew inspiration from the teaching of his predecessors, as well as from the many documents issued by bishops, from scientific studies promoted by members of the laity, from the work of Catholic movements and associations, and from the Church's practical achievements in the social field during the second half of the nineteenth century.

5. The "new things" to which the Pope devoted his attention were anything but positive. The first paragraph of the encyclical describes in strong terms the "new things" *(rerum novarum)* which gave it its name: "That *the spirit of revolutionary change* which has long been disturbing the nations of the world should have passed beyond the sphere of politics and made its influence felt in the related sphere of practical economics is not surprising. Progress in industry, the development of new trades, the changing relationship between employers and workers, the enormous wealth of a few as opposed to the poverty of the many, the increasing self-reliance of the workers and their closer association with each other, as well as a notable decline in morality: all these elements have led to the conflict now taking place."[8]

The Pope and the Church with him were confronted, as was the civil community, by a society which was torn by a conflict all the more harsh and inhumane because it knew no rule or regulation. It was *the conflict between capital and labor,* or — as the encyclical puts it — the worker question. It is precisely about this conflict, in the very pointed terms in which it then appeared, that the Pope did not hesitate to speak.

Here we find the first reflection for our times as suggested by the encyclical. In the face of a conflict which set man against man, almost as if they were "wolves," a conflict between the extremes of mere physical survival on the one side and opulence on the other, the Pope did not hesitate to intervene by virtue of his "apostolic office,"[9] that is, on the basis of the mission received from Jesus Christ himself to "feed his lambs and tend his sheep" (cf. Jn 21:15-17), and to "bind and loose" on earth for the kingdom of heaven (cf. Mt 16:19). The Pope's intention was certainly to restore peace, and the present-day reader cannot fail to note his severe condemnation, in no uncertain terms, of the class struggle.[10]

However, the Pope was very much aware that *peace is built on the foundation of justice:* what was essential to the encyclical was precisely its proclamation of the fundamental conditions for justice in the economic and social situation of the time.[11]

In this way, Pope Leo XIII, in the footsteps of his predecessors, created a lasting paradigm for the Church. The Church, in fact, has something to say about specific human situations, both individual and communal, national and international. She formulates a genuine doctrine for these situations, a *corpus* which enables her to analyze social realities, to make judgments about them and to indicate directions to be taken for the just resolution of the problems involved.

In Pope Leo XIII's time such a concept of the Church's right and duty was far from being commonly admitted. Indeed, a twofold approach prevailed: one directed to this world and this life, to which faith ought to remain extraneous; the other directed towards a purely other-worldly salvation, which neither enlightens nor directs existence on earth. The Pope's approach in publishing *Rerum Novarum* gave the Church "citizenship status" as it were, amid the changing realities of public life, and this standing would be more fully confirmed later on. In effect, to teach and to spread her social doctrine pertains to the Church's evangelizing mission and is an essential part of the Christian message, since this doctrine points out the direct consequences of that message in the life of society and situates daily work and struggles for justice in the context of bearing witness to Christ the Savior. This doctrine is likewise a source of unity and peace in dealing with the conflicts which inevitably arise in social and economic life. Thus it is possible to meet these new situations without degrading the human person's transcendent dignity, either in oneself or in one's adversaries, and to direct those situations towards just solutions.

Today, at a distance of a hundred years, the validity of this

11

approach affords me the opportunity to contribute to the development of Christian social doctrine. The "new evangelization," which the modern world urgently needs and which I have emphasized many times, must include among its essential elements *a proclamation of the Church's social doctrine.* As in the days of Pope Leo XIII, this doctrine is still suitable for indicating the right way to respond to the great challenges of today, when ideologies are being increasingly discredited. Now, as then, we need to repeat that there can be *no genuine solution of the "social question" apart from the Gospel,* and that the "new things" can find in the Gospel the context for their correct understanding and the proper moral perspective for judgment on them.

6. With the intention of shedding light on the *conflict* which had arisen between capital and labor, Pope Leo XIII affirmed the fundamental rights of workers. Indeed, the key to reading the encyclical is the *dignity of the worker* as such, and, for the same reason, the *dignity of work,* which is defined as follows: "to exert oneself for the sake of procuring what is necessary for the various purposes of life, and first of all for self-preservation."[12] The Pope describes work as "personal, inasmuch as the energy expended is bound up with the personality and is the exclusive property of him who acts, and, furthermore, was given to him for his advantage."[13] Work thus belongs to the vocation of every person; indeed, a human being expresses and fulfills himself by working. At the same time, work has a "social" dimension through its intimate relationship not only to the family, but also to the common good, since "it may truly be said that it is only by the labor of working-men that states grow rich."[14] These are themes that I have taken up and developed in my encyclical *Laborem Exercens.*[15]

Another important principle is undoubtedly that of the *right to "private property."*[16] The amount of space devoted to this subject in the encyclical shows the importance attached to it. The Pope is well aware that private property is not an absolute value, nor does he fail to proclaim the necessary complementary principles, such as the *universal destination of the earth's goods.*[17]

On the other hand, it is certainly true that the type of private property which Leo XIII mainly considers is land ownership.[18] But this does not mean that the reasons adduced to safeguard private property or to affirm the right to possess the things necessary for one's personal development and the development of one's family, whatever the concrete form which that right may assume, are not still valid today. This is something which must be affirmed once more in the face of the changes we are witnessing in systems formerly dominated by collective ownership of the means of production, as well as in the face of the increasing instances of poverty or, more precisely, of hindrances to private ownership in many parts of the world, including those where systems predominate which are based on an affirmation of the right to private property. As a result of these changes and of the persistence of poverty, a deeper analysis of the problem is called for, an analysis which will be developed later in this document.

7. In close connection with the right to private property, Pope Leo XIII's encyclical also affirms *other rights* as inalienable and proper to the human person. Prominent among these, because of the space which the Pope devotes to it and the importance which he attaches to it, is the "natural human right" to form private associations. This means above all *the right to establish professional associations* of employers and workers, or of workers alone.[19] Here we find the reason for the Church's defense and approval of the establishment of what are commonly called trade unions: certainly not because of ideological prejudices or in order to surrender to a class mentality, but because the right of association is a natural right of the human being, which therefore precedes his or her incorporation into political society. Indeed, the formation of unions "cannot...be prohibited by the State," because "the State is bound to protect natural rights, not to destroy them;

and if it forbids its citizens to form associations, it contradicts the very principle of its own existence."[20]

Together with this right, which — it must be stressed — the Pope explicitly acknowledges as belonging to workers, or, using his own language, to "the working class," the encyclical affirms just as clearly the right to the "limitation of working hours," the right to legitimate rest and the right of children and women[21] to be treated differently with regard to the type and duration of work.

If we keep in mind what history tells us about the practices permitted or at least not excluded by law regarding the way in which workers were employed, without any guarantees as to working hours or the hygienic conditions of the workplace, or even regarding the age and sex of apprentices, we can appreciate the Pope's severe statement: "It is neither just nor human so to grind men down with excessive labor as to stupefy their minds and wear out their bodies." And referring to the "contract" aimed at putting into effect "labor relations" of this sort, he affirms with greater precision that "in all agreements between employers and workers there is always the condition expressed or understood" that proper rest be allowed, proportionate to "the wear and tear of one's strength." He then concludes: "To agree in any other sense would be against what is right and just."[22]

8. The Pope immediately adds *another right* which the worker has as a person. This is the right to a "just wage," which cannot be left to the "free consent of the parties, so that the employer, having paid what was agreed upon, has done his part and seemingly is not called upon to do anything beyond."[23] It was said at the time that the State does not have the power to intervene in the terms of these contracts, except to ensure the fulfillment of what had been explicitly agreed upon. This concept of relations between employers and employees, purely pragmatic and inspired by a thoroughgoing individualism, is severely censured in the encyclical as contrary to the twofold nature of work as a

personal and necessary reality. For if work *as something personal* belongs to the sphere of the individual's free use of his own abilities and energy, *as something necessary* it is governed by the grave obligation of every individual to ensure "the preservation of life." "It necessarily follows," the Pope concludes, "that every individual has a natural right to procure what is required to live; and the poor can procure that in no other way than by what they can earn through their work."[24]

A workman's wages should be sufficient to enable him to support himself, his wife and his children. "If through necessity or fear of a worse evil the workman accepts harder conditions because an employer or contractor will afford no better, he is made the victim of force and injustice."[25]

Would that these words, written at a time when what has been called "unbridled capitalism" was pressing forward, should not have to be repeated today with the same severity. Unfortunately, even today one finds instances of contracts between employers and employees which lack reference to the most elementary justice regarding the employment of children or women, working hours, the hygienic condition of the workplace and fair pay; and this is the case despite the *international declarations* and *conventions* on the subject[26] and the *internal laws* of states. The Pope attributed to the "public authority" the "strict duty" of providing properly for the welfare of the workers, because a failure to do so violates justice; indeed, he did not hesitate to speak of "distributive justice."[27]

9. To these rights Pope Leo XIII adds another right regarding the condition of the working class, one which I wish to mention because of its importance: namely, the right to discharge freely one's religious duties. The Pope wished to proclaim this right within the context of the other rights and duties of workers, notwithstanding the general opinion, even in his day, that such questions pertained exclusively to an individual's private life. He

affirms the need for Sunday rest so that people may turn their thoughts to heavenly things and to the worship which they owe to Almighty God.[28] No one can take away this human right, which is based on a commandment; in the words of the Pope: "no man may with impunity violate that human dignity which God himself treats with great reverence," and consequently, the State must guarantee to the worker the exercise of this freedom.[29]

It would not be mistaken to see in this clear statement a springboard for the principle of the right to religious freedom, which was to become the subject of many solemn *international declarations* and *conventions,*[30] as well as of the Second Vatican Council's well-known *declaration* and of my own repeated teaching.[31] In this regard, one may ask whether existing laws and the practice of industrialized societies effectively ensure in our own day the exercise of this basic right to Sunday rest.

10. Another important aspect, which has many applications to our own day, is the concept of the relationship between the State and its citizens. *Rerum Novarum* criticizes two social and economic systems: socialism and liberalism. The opening section, in which the right to private property is reaffirmed, is devoted to socialism. Liberalism is not the subject of a special section, but it is worth noting that criticisms of it are raised in the treatment of the duties of the State.[32] The State cannot limit itself to "favoring one portion of the citizens," namely the rich and prosperous, nor can it "neglect the other," which clearly represents the majority of society. Otherwise, there would be a violation of that law of justice which ordains that every person should receive his due. "When there is question of defending the rights of individuals, the defenseless and the poor have a claim to special consideration. The richer class has many ways of shielding itself, and stands less in need of help from the State; whereas the mass of the poor have no resources of their own to fall back on, and must chiefly depend on the assistance of the State. It is for this reason that wage-

earners, since they mostly belong to the latter class, should be specially cared for and protected by the government."[33]

These passages are relevant today, especially in the face of the new forms of poverty in the world, and also because they are affirmations which do not depend on a specific notion of the State or on a particular political theory. Leo XIII is repeating an elementary principle of sound political organization, namely, the more that individuals are defenseless within a given society, the more they require the care and concern of others, and in particular the intervention of governmental authority.

In this way what we nowadays call the principle of solidarity, the validity of which both in the internal order of each nation and in the international order I have discussed in the encyclical *Sollicitudo Rei Socialis,*[34] is clearly seen to be one of the fundamental principles of the Christian view of social and political organization. This principle is frequently stated by Pope Leo XIII, who uses the term "friendship," a concept already found in Greek philosophy. Pope Pius XI refers to it with the equally meaningful term "social charity." Pope Paul VI, expanding the concept to cover the many modern aspects of the social question, speaks of a "civilization of love."[35]

11. Rereading the encyclical in the light of contemporary realities enables us to appreciate *the Church's constant concern for and dedication to* categories of people who are especially beloved to the Lord Jesus. The contents of the text is an excellent testimony to the continuity within the Church of the so-called "preferential option for the poor," an option which I defined as a "special form of primacy in the exercise of Christian charity."[36] Pope Leo's encyclical on the "condition of the workers" is thus an encyclical on the poor and on the terrible conditions to which the new and often violent process of industrialization had reduced great multitudes of people. Today, in many parts of the world, similar processes of economic, social and political transformation are creating the same evils.

If Pope Leo XIII calls upon the State to remedy the condition of the poor in accordance with justice, he does so because of his timely awareness that the State has the duty of watching over the common good and of ensuring that every sector of social life, not excluding the economic one, contributes to achieving that good, while respecting the rightful autonomy of each sector. This should not however lead us to think that Pope Leo expected the State to solve every social problem. On the contrary, he frequently insists on necessary limits to the State's intervention and on its instrumental character, inasmuch as the individual, the family and society are prior to the State, and inasmuch as the State exists in order to protect their rights and not stifle them.[37]

The relevance of these reflections for our own day is inescapable. It will be useful to return later to this important subject of the limits inherent in the nature of the State. For now, the points which have been emphasized (certainly not the only ones in the encyclical) are situated in continuity with the Church's social teaching, and in the light of a sound view of private property, work, the economic process, the reality of the State and, above all, of the person himself. Other themes will be mentioned later when we examine certain aspects of the contemporary situation. From this point forward it will be necessary to keep in mind that the main thread and, in a certain sense, the guiding principle of Pope Leo's encyclical, and of all of the Church's social doctrine, is a *correct view of the human person* and of the person's unique value, inasmuch as the human being "...is the only creature on earth which God willed for itself."[38] God has imprinted his own image and likeness on human beings (cf. Gen 1:26), conferring upon them an incomparable dignity, as the encyclical frequently insists. In effect, beyond the rights which one acquires by one's own work, there exist rights which do not correspond to any work performed, but which flow from one's essential dignity as a person.

Chapter II

Towards the "New Things" of Today

12. The commemoration of *Rerum Novarum* would be incomplete unless reference were also made to the situation of the world today. The document lends itself to such a reference, because the historical picture and the prognosis which it suggests have proved to be surprisingly accurate in the light of what has happened since then.

This is especially confirmed by the events which took place near the end of 1989 and at the beginning of 1990. These events, and the radical transformations which followed, can only be explained by the preceding situations which, to a certain extent, crystallized or institutionalized Leo XIII's predictions and the increasingly disturbing signs noted by his successors. Pope Leo foresaw the negative consequences — political, social and economic — of the social order proposed by "socialism," which at that time was still only a social philosophy and not yet a fully structured movement. It may seem surprising that "socialism" appeared at the beginning of the Pope's critique of solutions to the "question of the working class" at a time when "socialism" was not yet in the form of a strong and powerful State, with all the resources which that implies, as was later to happen. However, he correctly judged the danger posed to the masses by the attractive presentation of this simple and radical solution to the "question of the working class" of the time — all the more so when one considers the terrible situation of injustice in which the working classes of the recently industrialized nations found themselves.

Two things must be emphasized here: first, the great clarity in perceiving, in all its harshness, the actual condition of the working class — men, women and children; secondly, equal clarity in recognizing the evil of a solution which, by appearing to reverse the positions of the poor and the rich, was in reality detrimental to the very people whom it was meant to help. The remedy would prove worse than the sickness. By defining the nature of the socialism of his day as the suppression of private property, Leo XIII arrived at the crux of the problem.

His words deserve to be reread attentively: "To remedy these wrongs [the unjust distribution of wealth and the poverty of the workers], the socialists encourage the poor man's envy of the rich and strive to do away with private property, contending that individual possessions should become the common property of all...; but their contentions are so clearly powerless to end the controversy that, were they carried into effect, the working man himself would be among the first to suffer. They are moreover emphatically unjust, for they would rob the lawful possessor, distort the functions of the State, and create utter confusion in the community."[39] The evils caused by the setting up of this type of socialism as a state system — what would later be called "Real Socialism" — could not be better expressed.

13. Continuing our reflections, and referring also to what has been said in the encyclicals *Laborem Exercens* and *Sollicitudo Rei Socialis,* we have to add that the fundamental error of socialism is anthropological in nature. Socialism considers the individual person simply as an element, a molecule within the social organism, so that the good of the individual is completely subordinated to the functioning of the socio-economic mechanism. Socialism likewise maintains that the good of the individual can be realized without reference to his free choice, to the

unique and exclusive responsibility which he exercises in the face of good or evil. Man is thus reduced to a series of social relationships, and the concept of the person as the autonomous subject of moral decision disappears, the very subject whose decisions build the social order. From this mistaken conception of the person there arise both a distortion of law, which defines the sphere of the exercise of freedom, and an opposition to private property. A person who is deprived of something he can call "his own," and of the possibility of earning a living through his own initiative, comes to depend on the social machine and on those who control it. This makes it much more difficult for him to recognize his dignity as a person, and hinders progress towards the building up of an authentic human community.

In contrast, from the Christian vision of the human person there necessarily follows a correct picture of society. According to *Rerum Novarum* and the whole social doctrine of the Church, the social nature of man is not completely fulfilled in the State, but is realized in various intermediary groups, beginning with the family and including economic, social, political and cultural groups which stem from human nature itself and have their own autonomy, always with a view to the common good. This is what I have called the "subjectivity" of society which, together with the subjectivity of the individual, was cancelled out by "Real Socialism."[40]

If we then inquire as to the source of this mistaken concept of the nature of the person and the "subjectivity" of society, we must reply that its first cause is atheism. It is by responding to the call of God contained in the being of things that man becomes aware of his transcendent dignity. Every individual must give this response, which constitutes the apex of his humanity, and no social mechanism or collective subject can substitute for it. The denial of God deprives the person of his foundation, and consequently leads to a reorganization of the social order without reference to the person's dignity and responsibility.

The atheism of which we are speaking is also closely connected with the rationalism of the Enlightenment, which views human and social reality in a mechanistic way. Thus there is a denial of the supreme insight concerning man's true greatness, his transcendence in respect to earthly realities, the contradiction in his heart between the desire for the fullness of what is good and his own inability to attain it and, above all, the need for salvation which results from this situation.

14. From the same atheistic source, socialism also derives its choice of the means of action condemned in *Rerum Novarum,* namely, class struggle. The Pope does not, of course, intend to condemn every possible form of social conflict. The Church is well aware that in the course of history conflicts of interest between different social groups inevitably arise, and that in the face of such conflicts Christians must often take a position, honestly and decisively. The encyclical *Laborem Exercens* moreover clearly recognized the positive role of conflict when it takes the form of a "struggle for social justice";[41] *Quadragesimo Anno* had already stated that "if the class struggle abstains from enmities and mutual hatred, it gradually changes into an honest discussion of differences founded on a desire for justice."[42]

However, what is condemned in class struggle is the idea that conflict is not restrained by ethical or juridical considerations, or by respect for the dignity of others (and consequently of oneself); a reasonable compromise is thus excluded, and what is pursued is not the general good of society, but a partisan interest which replaces the common good and sets out to destroy whatever stands in its way. In a word, it is a question of transferring to the sphere of internal conflict between social groups the doctrine of "total war," which the militarism and imperialism of that time brought to bear on international relations. As a result of this doctrine, the search for a proper balance between the interests of the various nations was replaced by attempts to impose the absolute domination of one's own side through the destruction of the other side's capacity to resist, using every possible means, not excluding the use of lies, terror tactics against citizens, and weapons of utter destruction (which precisely in those years were beginning to be designed). Therefore class struggle in the Marxist sense and militarism have the same root, namely, atheism and contempt for the human person, which place the principle of force above that of reason and law.

15. *Rerum Novarum* is opposed to state control of the means of production, which would reduce every citizen to being a "cog" in the state machine. It is no less forceful in criticizing a concept of the State which completely excludes the economic sector from the State's range of interest and action. There is certainly a legitimate sphere of autonomy in economic life which the State should not enter. The State, however, has the task of determining the juridical framework within which economic affairs are to be conducted, and thus of safeguarding the prerequisites of a free economy, which presumes a certain equality between the parties, such that one party would not be so powerful as practically to reduce the other to subservience.[43]

In this regard, *Rerum Novarum* points the way to just reforms which can restore dignity to work as the free activity of man. These reforms imply that society and the State will both assume responsibility, especially for protecting the worker from the nightmare of unemployment. Historically, this has happened in two converging ways: either through economic policies aimed at ensuring balanced growth and full employment, or through unemployment insurance and re-training programs capable of ensuring a smooth transfer of workers from crisis sectors to those in expansion.

Furthermore, society and the State must ensure wage levels adequate for the maintenance of the worker and his family, including a certain amount for savings. This requires a continuous effort to improve workers' training and capability so that their work will be more skilled and productive, as well as careful controls and adequate legislative measures to block shameful forms of exploitation, especially to the disadvantage of the most vulnerable workers, of immigrants and of those on the margins of society. The role of trade unions in negotiating minimum salaries and working conditions is decisive in this area.

Finally, "humane" working hours and adequate free-time need to be guaranteed, as well as the right to express one's own personality at the workplace without suffering any affront to one's conscience or personal dignity. This is the place to mention once more the role of trade unions, not only in negotiating contracts, but also as "places" where workers can express themselves. They serve the development of an authentic culture of work and help workers to share in a fully human way in the life of their place of employment.[44]

The State must contribute to the achievement of these goals both directly and indirectly. Indirectly and according to the *principle of subsidiarity,* by creating favorable conditions for the free exercise of economic activity, which will lead to abundant opportunities for employment and sources of wealth. Directly and according to the *principle of solidarity,* by defending the weakest, by placing certain limits on the autonomy of the parties who determine working conditions, and by ensuring in every case the necessary minimum support for the unemployed worker.[45]

The encyclical and the related social teaching of the Church had far-reaching influence in the years bridging the nineteenth and twentieth centuries. This influence is evident in the numerous reforms which were introduced in the areas of social security, pensions, health insurance and compensation in the case of accidents, within the framework of greater respect for the rights of workers.[46]

16. These reforms were carried out in part by states, but in the struggle to achieve them *the role of the workers' movement* was an important one. This movement, which began as a response of moral conscience to unjust and harmful situations, conducted a widespread campaign for reform, far removed from vague ideology and closer to the daily needs of workers. In this context its efforts were often joined to those of Christians in order to improve workers' living conditions. Later on, this movement was dominated to a certain extent by the Marxist ideology against which *Rerum Novarum* had spoken.

These same reforms were also partly the result *of an open process by which society organized itself* through the establishment of effective instruments of solidarity, which were capable of sustaining an economic growth more respectful of the values of the person. Here we should remember the numerous efforts to which Christians made a notable contribution in establishing producers', consumers' and credit cooperatives, in promoting general education and professional training, in experimenting with various forms of participation in the life of the workplace and in the life of society in general.

Thus, as we look at the past, there is good reason to thank God that the great encyclical was not without an echo in human hearts and indeed led to a generous response on the practical level. Still, we must acknowledge that its prophetic message was not fully accepted by people at the time. Precisely for this reason there ensued some very serious tragedies.

17. Reading the encyclical within the context of Pope Leo's whole magisterium,[47] we see how it points essentially to the socio-economic consequences of an error which has even greater implications. As has been mentioned, this error consists in an understanding of human freedom which detaches it from obedience to the truth, and consequently from the duty to respect the rights of others. The essence of freedom then becomes self-love

carried to the point of contempt for God and neighbor, a self-love which leads to an unbridled affirmation of self-interest and which refuses to be limited by any demand of justice.[48]

This very error had extreme consequences in the tragic series of wars which ravaged Europe and the world between 1914 and 1945. Some of these resulted from militarism and exaggerated nationalism, and from related forms of totalitarianism; some derived from the class struggle; still others were civil wars or wars of an ideological nature. Without the terrible burden of hatred and resentment which had built up as a result of so many injustices both on the international level and within individual states, such cruel wars would not have been possible, in which great nations invested their energies and in which there was no hesitation to violate the most sacred human rights, with the extermination of entire peoples and social groups being planned and carried out. Here we recall the Jewish people in particular, whose terrible fate has become a symbol of the aberration of which man is capable when he turns against God.

However, it is only when hatred and injustice are sanctioned and organized by the ideologies based on them, rather than on the truth about the human person, that they take possession of entire nations and drive them to act.[49] *Rerum Novarum* opposed ideologies of hatred and showed how violence and resentment could be overcome by justice. May the memory of those terrible events guide the actions of everyone, particularly the leaders of nations in our own time, when other forms of injustice are fuelling new hatreds and when new ideologies which exalt violence are appearing on the horizon.

18. While it is true that since 1945 weapons have been silent on the European continent, it must be remembered that true peace is never simply the result of military victory, but rather implies both the removal of the causes of war and genuine reconciliation between peoples. For many years there has been in Europe and the

world a situation of non-war rather than genuine peace. Half of the continent fell under the domination of a Communist dictatorship, while the other half organized itself in defense against this threat. Many peoples lost the ability to control their own destiny and were enclosed within the suffocating boundaries of an empire in which efforts were made to destroy their historical memory and the centuries-old roots of their culture. As a result of this violent division of Europe, enormous masses of people were compelled to leave their homeland or were forcibly deported.

An insane arms race swallowed up the resources needed for the development of national economies and for assistance to the less developed nations. Scientific and technological progress, which should have contributed to man's well-being, was transformed into an instrument of war: science and technology were directed to the production of ever more efficient and destructive weapons. Meanwhile, an ideology, a perversion of authentic philosophy, was called upon to provide doctrinal justification for the new war. And this war was not simply expected and prepared for, but was actually fought with enormous bloodshed in various parts of the world. The logic of power blocs or empires, denounced in various Church documents and recently in the encyclical *Sollicitudo Rei Socialis,*[50] led to a situation in which controversies and disagreements among Third World countries were systematically aggravated and exploited in order to create difficulties for the adversary.

Extremist groups, seeking to resolve such controversies through the use of arms, found ready political and military support and were equipped and trained for war; those who tried to find peaceful and humane solutions, with respect for the legitimate interests of all parties, remained isolated and often fell victim to their opponents. In addition, the precariousness of the peace which followed the Second World War was one of the principal causes of the militarization of many Third World countries and the fratricidal conflicts which afflicted them, as well as of the spread of terrorism and of increasingly barbaric means of political and military conflict. Moreover, the whole world was oppressed by the threat of an atomic war capable of leading to the extinction of humanity. Science used for military purposes had placed this decisive instrument at the disposal of hatred, strengthened by ideology. But if war can end without winners or losers in a suicide of humanity, then we must repudiate the logic which leads to it: the idea that the effort to destroy the enemy, confrontation and war itself are factors of progress and historical advancement.[51] When the need for this repudiation is understood, the concepts of "total war" and "class struggle" must necessarily be called into question.

19. At the end of the Second World War, however, such a development was still being formed in people's consciences. What received attention was the spread of Communist totalitarianism over more than half of Europe and over other parts of the world. The war, which should have reestablished freedom and restored the right of nations, ended without having attained these goals. Indeed, in a way, for many peoples, especially those which had suffered most during the war, it openly contradicted these goals. It may be said that the situation which arose has evoked different responses.

Following the destruction caused by the war, we see in some countries and under certain aspects a positive effort to rebuild a democratic society inspired by social justice, so as to deprive Communism of the revolutionary potential represented by masses of people subjected to exploitation and oppression. In general, such attempts endeavor to preserve free market mechanisms, ensuring, by means of a stable currency and the harmony of social relations, the conditions for steady and healthy economic growth in which people through their own work can build a better future for themselves and their families. At the same time, these attempts try to avoid making market mechanisms the only point of reference for social life, and they tend to subject them to public control which upholds the principle of the common destination of material goods. In this context, an abundance of work opportunities, a solid system of social security and professional training, the freedom to join trade unions and the effective action of unions, the assistance provided in cases of unemployment, the opportunities for democratic participation in the life of society – all these are meant to deliver work from the mere condition of "a commodity," and to guarantee its dignity.

Then there are the other social forces and ideological movements which oppose Marxism by setting up systems of "national security," aimed at controlling the whole of society in a systematic way, in order to make Marxist infiltration impossible. By emphasizing and increasing the power of the State, they wish to protect their people from Communism, but in doing so they run the grave risk of destroying the freedom and values of the person, the very things for whose sake it is necessary to oppose Communism.

Another kind of response, practical in nature, is represented by the affluent society or the consumer society. It seeks to defeat Marxism on the level of pure materialism by showing how a free-market society can achieve a greater satisfaction of material human needs than Communism, while equally excluding spiritual values. In reality, while on the one hand it is true that this social model shows the failure of Marxism to contribute to a humane and better society, on the other hand, insofar as it denies an autonomous existence and value to morality, law, culture and religion, it agrees with Marxism, in the sense that it totally reduces man to the sphere of economics and the satisfaction of material needs.

20. During the same period a widespread process of "decolonization" occurred, by which many countries gained or regained their independence and the right freely to determine their own destiny. With the formal reacquisition of state sovereignty,

however, these countries often find themselves merely at the beginning of the journey towards the construction of genuine independence. Decisive sectors of the economy still remain *de facto* in the hands of large foreign companies which are unwilling to commit themselves to the long-term development of the host country. Political life itself is controlled by foreign powers, while within the national boundaries there are tribal groups not yet amalgamated into a genuine national community. Also lacking is a class of competent professional people capable of running the state apparatus in an honest and just way, nor are there qualified personnel for managing the economy in an efficient and responsible manner.

Given this situation, many think that Marxism can offer a sort of shortcut for building up the nation and the State; thus many variants of socialism emerge with specific national characteristics. Legitimate demands for national recovery, forms of nationalism and also of militarism, principles drawn from ancient popular traditions (which are sometimes in harmony with Christian social doctrine) and Marxist-Leninist concepts and ideas — all these mingle in the many ideologies which take shape in ways that differ from case to case.

21. Lastly, it should be remembered that after the Second World War, and in reaction to its horrors, there arose a more lively sense of human rights, which found recognition in a number of *international documents*[52] and, one might say, in the drawing up of a new "right of nations," to which the Holy See has constantly contributed. The focal point of this evolution has been the United Nations Organization. Not only has there been a development in awareness of the rights of individuals, but also in awareness of the rights of nations, as well as a clearer realization of the need to act in order to remedy the grave imbalances that exist between the various geographical areas of the world. In a certain sense, these imbalances have shifted the center of the social question from the national to the international level.[53]

While noting this process with satisfaction, nevertheless one cannot ignore the fact that the overall balance of the various policies of aid for development has not always been positive. The United Nations, moreover, has not yet succeeded in establishing, as alternatives to war, effective means for the resolution of international conflicts. This seems to be the most urgent problem which the international community has yet to resolve.

Chapter III

The Year 1989

22. It is on the basis of the world situation just described, and already elaborated in the encyclical *Sollicitudo Rei Socialis,* that the unexpected and promising significance of the events of recent years can be understood. Although they certainly reached their climax in 1989 in the countries of Central and Eastern Europe, they embrace a longer period of time and a wider geographical area. In the course of the 80s, certain dictatorial and oppressive regimes fell one by one in some countries of Latin America and also of Africa and Asia. In other cases there began a difficult but productive transition towards more participatory and more just political structures. An important, even decisive, contribution was made by *the Church's commitment to defend and promote human rights.* In situations strongly influenced by ideology, in which polarization obscured the awareness of a human dignity common to all, the Church affirmed clearly and forcefully that every individual — whatever his or her personal convictions — bears the image of God and therefore deserves respect. Often, the vast majority of people identified themselves with this kind of affirmation, and this led to a search for forms of protest and for political solutions more respectful of the dignity of the person.

From this historical process new forms of democracy have emerged which offer a hope for change in fragile political and social structures weighed down by a painful series of injustices and resentments, as well as by a heavily damaged economy and serious social conflicts. Together with the whole Church, I thank God for the often heroic witness borne in such difficult circumstances by many pastors, entire Christian communities, individual members of the faithful, and other people of good will; at the same time I pray that he will sustain the efforts being made by everyone to build a better future. This is, in fact, a responsibility which falls not only to the citizens of the countries in question, but to all Christians and people of good will. It is a question of showing that the complex problems faced by those peoples can be resolved through dialogue and solidarity, rather than by a struggle to destroy the enemy through war.

23. Among the many factors involved in the fall of oppressive regimes, some deserve special mention. Certainly, the decisive factor which gave rise to the changes was the violation of the rights of workers. It cannot be forgotten that the fundamental crisis of systems claiming to express the rule and indeed the dictatorship of the working class began with the great upheavals which took place in Poland in the name of solidarity. It was the throngs of working people which foreswore the ideology which presumed to speak in their name. On the basis of a hard, lived experience of work and of oppression, it was they who recovered and, in a sense, rediscovered the content and principles of the Church's social doctrine.

Also worthy of emphasis is the fact that the fall of this kind of "bloc" or empire was accomplished almost everywhere by means of peaceful protest, using only the weapons of truth and justice. While Marxism held that only by exacerbating social conflicts was it possible to resolve them through violent confrontation, the protests which led to the collapse of Marxism tenaciously insisted on trying every avenue of negotiation, dialogue, and witness to the truth, appealing to the conscience of the adversary and seeking to reawaken in him a sense of shared human dignity.

It seemed that the European order resulting from the Second World War and sanctioned by the *Yalta Agreements* could only be overturned by another war. Instead, it has been overcome by the non-violent commitment of people who, while always refusing to yield to the force of power, succeeded time after time in finding effective ways of bearing witness to the truth. This disarmed the adversary, since violence always needs to justify itself through deceit, and to appear, however falsely, to be defending a right or responding to a threat posed by others.[54] Once again I thank God for having sustained people's hearts amid difficult trials, and I pray that this example will prevail in other places and other circumstances. May people learn to fight for justice without violence, renouncing class struggle in their internal disputes, and war in international ones.

24. The second factor in the crisis was certainly the inefficiency of the economic system, which is not to be considered simply as a technical problem, but rather a consequence of the violation of the human rights to private initiative, to ownership of property and to freedom in the economic sector. To this must be added the cultural and national dimension: it is not possible to understand the human person on the basis of economics alone, nor to define the person simply on the basis of class membership. A human being is understood in a more complete way when situated within the sphere of culture through language, history, and the position one takes towards the fundamental events of life, such as birth, love, work and death. At the heart of every culture lies the attitude a person takes to the greatest mystery: the mystery of God. Different cultures are basically different ways of facing the question of the meaning of personal existence. When this question is eliminated, the culture and moral life of nations are corrupted. For this reason the struggle to defend work was spontaneously linked to the struggle for culture and for national rights.

But the true cause of the new developments was the spiritual void brought about by atheism, which deprived the younger generations of a sense of direction and in many cases led them, in the irrepressible search for personal identity and for the meaning of life, to rediscover the religious roots of their national cultures, and to rediscover the person of Christ himself as the existentially adequate response to the desire in every human heart for goodness, truth and life. This search was supported by the witness of those who, in difficult circumstances and under persecution, remained faithful to God. Marxism had promised to uproot the need for God from the human heart, but the results have shown that it is not possible to succeed in this without throwing the heart into turmoil.

25. The events of 1989 are an example of the success of willingness to negotiate and of the Gospel spirit in the face of an adversary determined not to be bound by moral principles. These events are a warning to those who, in the name of political realism, wish to banish law and morality from the political arena. Undoubtedly, the struggle which led to the changes of 1989 called for clarity, moderation, suffering and sacrifice. In a certain sense, it was a struggle born of prayer, and it would have been unthinkable without immense trust in God, the Lord of history, who carries the human heart in his hands. It is by uniting their own sufferings for the sake of truth and freedom to the sufferings of Christ on the cross that people are able to accomplish the miracle of peace and are in a position to discern the often narrow path between the cowardice which gives in to evil and the violence which, under the illusion of fighting evil, only makes it worse.

Nevertheless, it cannot be forgotten that the manner in which the individual exercises freedom is conditioned in innumerable ways. While these certainly have an influence on freedom, they do not determine it; they make the exercise of freedom more difficult or less difficult, but they cannot destroy it. Not only is it wrong from the ethical point of view to disregard human nature, which is made for freedom, but in practice it is impossible to do so. Where society is so organized as to reduce arbitrarily or even suppress the sphere in which freedom is legitimately exercised, the result is that the life of society becomes progressively disorganized and goes into decline.

Moreover, humankind, created for freedom, bears within itself the wound of original sin, which constantly draws persons toward evil and puts them in need of redemption. Not only is *this doctrine an integral part of Christian revelation;* it also has great hermeneutical value insofar as it helps one to understand human reality. The human person tends towards good, but is also capable of evil. One can transcend one's immediate interest and still remain bound to it. The social order will be all the more stable, the more it takes this fact into account and does not place in opposition personal interest and the interests of society as a whole, but rather seeks ways to bring them into fruitful harmony. In fact, where self-interest is violently suppressed, it is replaced by a burdensome system of bureaucratic control which dries up the wellsprings of initiative and creativity. When people think they possess the secret of a perfect social organization which makes evil impossible, they also think that they can use any means, including violence and deceit, in order to bring that organization into being. Politics then becomes a "secular religion" which operates under the illusion of creating paradise in this world. But no political society—which possesses its own autonomy and laws[55]—can ever be confused with the Kingdom of God. The Gospel parable of the weeds among the wheat (cf. Mt 13:24-30; 36-43) teaches that it is for God alone to separate the subjects of the Kingdom from the subjects of the Evil One, and that this judgment will take place at the end of time. By presuming to anticipate judgment here and now, people put themselves in the place of God and set themselves against the patience of God.

Through Christ's sacrifice on the cross, the victory of the

Kingdom of God has been achieved once and for all. Nevertheless, the Christian life involves a struggle against temptation and the forces of evil. Only at the end of history will the Lord return in glory for the final judgment (cf. Mt 25:31) with the establishment of a new heaven and a new earth (cf. 2 Pt 3:13; Rev 21:1); but as long as time lasts the struggle between good and evil continues even in the human heart itself.

What Sacred Scripture teaches us about the prospects of the Kingdom of God is not without consequences for the life of temporal societies, which, as the adjective indicates, belong to the realm of time, with all that this implies of imperfection and impermanence. The Kingdom of God, being *in* the world without being *of* the world, throws light on the order of human society, while the power of grace penetrates that order and gives it life. In this way the requirements of a society worthy of man are better perceived, deviations are corrected, the courage to work for what is good is reinforced. In union with all people of good will, Christians, especially the laity, are called to this task of imbuing human realities with the Gospel.[56]

26. The events of 1989 took place principally in the countries of Eastern and Central Europe. However, they have worldwide importance because they have positive and negative consequences which concern the whole human family. These consequences are not mechanistic or fatalistic in character, but rather are opportunities for human freedom to cooperate with the merciful plan of God who acts within history.

The first consequence was *an encounter* in some countries *between the Church and the workers' movement,* which came about as a result of an ethical and explicitly Christian reaction against a widespread situation of injustice. For about a century the workers' movement had fallen in part under the dominance of Marxism, in the conviction that the working class, in order to struggle effectively against oppression, had to appropriate its economic and materialistic theories.

In the crisis of Marxism, the natural dictates of the consciences of workers have reemerged in a demand for justice and a recognition of the dignity of work, in conformity with the social doctrine of the Church.[57] The worker movement is part of a more general movement among workers and other people of good will for the liberation of the human person and for the affirmation of human rights. It is a movement which today has spread to many countries, and which, far from opposing the Catholic Church, looks to her with interest.

The crisis of Marxism does not rid the world of the situations of injustice and oppression which Marxism itself exploited and on which it fed. To those who are searching today for a new and authentic theory and praxis of liberation, the Church offers not only her social doctrine and, in general, her teaching about the human person redeemed in Christ, but also her concrete commitment and material assistance in the struggle against marginalization and suffering.

In the recent past, the sincere desire to be on the side of the oppressed and not to be cut off from the course of history has led many believers to seek in various ways an impossible compromise between Marxism and Christianity. Moving beyond all that was short-lived in these attempts, present circumstances are leading to a reaffirmation of the positive value of an authentic theology of integral human liberation.[58] Considered from this point of view, the events of 1989 are proving to be important also for the countries of the Third World, which are searching for their own path to development, just as they were important for the countries of Central and Eastern Europe.

27. The second consequence concerns the peoples of Europe themselves. Many individual, social, regional and national injustices were committed during and prior to the years in which Communism dominated; much hatred and ill will have accumulated. There is a real danger that these will re-explode after the

collapse of dictatorship, provoking serious conflicts and casualties, should there be a lessening of the moral commitment and conscious striving to bear witness to the truth which were the inspiration for past efforts. It is to be hoped that hatred and violence will not triumph in people's hearts, especially among those who are struggling for justice, and that all people will grow in the spirit of peace and forgiveness.

What is needed are concrete steps to create or consolidate international structures capable of intervening through appropriate arbitration in the conflicts which arise between nations, so that each nation can uphold its own rights and reach a just agreement and peaceful settlement vis-à-vis the rights of others. This is especially needed for the nations of Europe, which are closely united in a bond of common culture and an age-old history. A great effort is needed to rebuild morally and economically the countries which have abandoned Communism. For a long time the most elementary economic relationships were distorted, and basic virtues of economic life, such as truthfulness, trustworthiness and hard work were denigrated. A patient material and moral reconstruction is needed, even as people, exhausted by longstanding privation, are asking their governments for tangible and immediate results in the form of material benefits and an adequate fulfillment of their legitimate aspirations.

The fall of Marxism has naturally had a great impact on the division of the planet into worlds which are closed to one another and in jealous competition. It has further highlighted the reality of interdependence among peoples, as well as the fact that human work, by its nature, is meant to unite peoples, not divide them. Peace and prosperity, in fact, are goods which belong to the whole human race: it is not possible to enjoy them in a proper and lasting way if they are achieved and maintained at the cost of other peoples and nations, by violating their rights or excluding them from the sources of well-being.

28. In a sense, for some countries of Europe the real post-war period is just beginning. The radical reordering of economic systems, hitherto collectivized, entails problems and sacrifices comparable to those which the countries of Western Europe had to face in order to rebuild after the Second World War. It is right that in the present difficulties the formerly Communist countries should be aided by the united effort of other nations. Obviously they themselves must be the primary agents of their own development, but they must also be given a reasonable opportunity to accomplish this goal, something that cannot happen without the help of other countries. Moreover, their present condition, marked by difficulties and shortages, is the result of an historical process in which the formerly Communist countries were often objects and not subjects. Thus they find themselves in the present situation not as a result of free choice or mistakes which were made, but as a consequence of tragic historical events which were violently imposed on them, and which prevented them from following the path of economic and social development.

Assistance from other countries, especially the countries of Europe which were part of that history and which bear responsibility for it, represents a debt in justice. But it also corresponds to the interest and welfare of Europe as a whole, since Europe cannot live in peace if the various conflicts which have arisen as a result of the past are to become more acute because of a situation of economic disorder, spiritual dissatisfaction and desperation.

This need, however, must not lead to a slackening of efforts to sustain and assist the countries of the Third World, which often suffer even more serious conditions of poverty and want.[59] What is called for is a special effort to mobilize resources, which are not lacking in the world as a whole, for the purpose of economic growth and common development, redefining the priorities and hierarchies of values on the basis of which economic and political choices are made. Enormous resources can be made available by disarming the huge military machines which were constructed for the conflict between East and West. These resources could become even more abundant if, in place of war, reliable procedures for the resolution of conflicts could be set up, with the resulting spread of the principle of arms control and arms reduction, also in the countries of the Third World, through the adoption of appropriate measures against the arms trade.[60] But it will be necessary above all to abandon a mentality in which the poor — as individuals and as peoples — are considered a burden, as irksome intruders trying to consume what others have produced. The poor ask for the right to share in enjoying material goods and to make good use of their capacity for work, thus creating a world that is more just and prosperous for all. The advancement of the poor constitutes a great opportunity for the moral, cultural and even economic growth of all humanity.

29. Finally, development must not be understood solely in economic terms, but in a way that is fully human.[61] It is not only a question of raising all peoples to the level currently enjoyed by the richest countries, but rather of building up a more decent life through united labor, of concretely enhancing every individual's dignity and creativity, as well as his capacity to respond to his personal vocation, and thus to God's call. The apex of development is the exercise of the right and duty to seek God, to know him and to live in accordance with that knowledge.[62] In the totalitarian and authoritarian regimes, the principle that force predominates over reason was carried to the extreme. A person was compelled to submit to a conception of reality imposed on him by coercion, and not reached by virtue of his own reason and the exercise of his own freedom. This principle must be overturned and total recognition must be given to *the rights of the human conscience,* which is bound only to the truth, both natural and revealed. The recognition of these rights represents the primary foundation of every authentically free political order.[63] It is important to reaffirm this latter principle for several reasons:

a) because the old forms of totalitarianism and authoritarianism are not yet completely vanquished; indeed there is a risk that they will regain their strength. This demands renewed efforts of cooperation and solidarity between all countries;

b) because in the developed countries there is sometimes an excessive promotion of purely utilitarian values, with an appeal to the appetites and inclinations towards immediate gratification, making it difficult to recognize and respect the hierarchy of the true values of human existence;

c) because in some countries new forms of religious fundamentalism are emerging which covertly, or even openly, deny to citizens of faiths other than that of the majority the full exercise of their civil and religious rights, preventing them from taking part in the cultural process, and restricting both the Church's right to preach the Gospel and the rights of those who hear this preaching to accept it and to be converted to Christ. No authentic progress is possible without respect for the natural and fundamental right to know the truth and live according to that truth. The exercise and development of this right includes the right to discover and freely to accept Jesus Christ, who is humanity's true good.[64]

Chapter IV

Private Property and the Universal Destination of Material Goods

30. In *Rerum Novarum,* Leo XIII strongly affirmed the natural character of the right to private property, using various arguments against the socialism of his time.[65] This right, which is fundamental for the autonomy and development of the person, has always been defended by the Church up to our own day. At the same time, the Church teaches that the possession of material goods is not an absolute right, and that its limits are inscribed in its very nature as a human right.

While the Pope proclaimed the right to private ownership, he affirmed with equal clarity that the "use" of goods, while marked by freedom, is subordinated to their original common destination as created goods, as well as to the will of Jesus Christ as expressed in the Gospel. Pope Leo wrote: "those whom fortune favors are admonished...that they should tremble at the warnings of Jesus Christ...and that a most strict account must be given to the Supreme Judge for the use of all they possess"; and quoting Saint Thomas Aquinas, he added: "But if the question be asked, how must one's possessions be used? the Church replies without hesitation that man should not consider his material possessions as his own, but as common to all...," because "above the laws and judgments of men stands the law, the judgment of Christ."[66]

The Successors of Leo XIII have repeated this twofold affirmation: the necessity and therefore the legitimacy of private ownership, as well as the limits which are imposed on it.[67] The Second Vatican Council likewise clearly restated the traditional doctrine in words which bear repeating: "In making use of the exterior things we lawfully possess, we ought to regard them not just as our own but also as common, in the sense that they can profit not only the owners but others too"; and a little later we read: "Private property or some ownership of external goods affords each person the scope needed for personal and family autonomy, and should be regarded as an extension of human freedom.... Of its nature private property also has a social function which is based on the law of the *common purpose of goods*."[68] I have returned to this same doctrine, first in my address to the Third Conference of the Latin American Bishops at Puebla, and later in the encyclicals *Laborem Exercens* and *Sollicitudo Rei Socialis*.[69]

31. Rereading this teaching on the right to property and the common destination of material wealth as it applies to the present time, the question can be raised concerning the origin of the material goods which sustain human life, satisfy people's needs and are an object of their rights.

The original source of all that is good is the very act of God, who created both the earth and humankind, and who gave the earth to humankind, so that we might have dominion over it by our work and enjoy its fruits (Gen 1:28). God gave the earth to the whole human race for the sustenance of all its members, without excluding or favoring anyone. This is *the foundation of the universal destination of the earth's goods*. The earth, by reason of its fruitfulness and its capacity to satisfy human needs, is God's first gift for the sustenance of human life. But the earth does not yield its fruits without a particular human response to God's gift, that is to say, without work. It is through work that we, using our intelligence and exercising our freedom, succeed in dominating the earth and making it a fitting home. In this way, one makes part of the earth one's own, precisely the part which one has acquired through work; this is *the origin of individual property*. Obviously, one also has the responsibility not to hinder others from having their own part of God's gift; indeed, one must cooperate with others so that together all can dominate the earth.

In history, these two factors — *work* and *the land* — are to be found at the beginning of every human society. However, they do not always stand in the same relationship to each other. At one time *the natural fruitfulness of the earth* appeared to be, and was in fact, the primary factor of wealth, while work was, as it were, the help and support for this fruitfulness. In our time, *the role of human work* is becoming increasingly important as the productive factor both of nonmaterial and of material wealth. Moreover, it is becoming clearer how a person's work is naturally interrelated with the work of others. More than ever, work is *work with others* and *work for others:* it is a matter of doing something for someone else. Work becomes ever more fruitful and productive to the extent that people become more knowledgeable of the productive potentialities of the earth and more profoundly cognizant of the needs of those for whom their work is done.

32. In our time, in particular, there exists another form of ownership which is becoming no less important than land: *the possession of know-how, technology and skill.* The wealth of the industrialized nations is based much more on this kind of ownership than on natural resources.

Mention has just been made of the fact that *people work with each other,* sharing in a "community of work" which embraces ever widening circles. A person who produces something other than for his own use generally does so in order that others may use it after they have paid a just price, mutually agreed upon through free bargaining. It is precisely the ability to foresee both the needs of others and the combinations of productive factors most adapted to satisfying those needs that constitutes another important source of wealth in modern society. Besides, many goods cannot be adequately produced through the work of an isolated individual; they require the cooperation of many people in working towards a common goal. Organizing such a productive effort, planning its duration in time, making sure that it corresponds in a positive way to the demands which it must satisfy, and taking the necessary risks — all this too is a source of wealth in today's society. In this way, the *role* of disciplined and creative *human work* and, as an essential part of that work, *initiative and entrepreneurial ability* becomes increasingly evident and decisive.[70]

This process, which throws practical light on a truth about the person which Christianity has constantly affirmed, should be viewed carefully and favorably. Indeed, besides the earth, humankind's principal resource is *the person himself.* His intelligence enables him to discover the earth's productive potential and the many different ways in which human needs can be satisfied. It is his disciplined work in close collaboration with others that makes possible the creation of ever more extensive *working communities* which can be relied upon to transform natural and human environments. Important virtues are involved in this process, such as diligence, industriousness, prudence in undertaking reasonable risks, reliability and fidelity in interpersonal relationships, as well as courage in carrying out decisions which are difficult and painful but necessary, both for the overall working of a business and in meeting possible setbacks.

The modern *business economy* has positive aspects. Its basis is human freedom exercised in the economic field, just as it is exercised in many other fields. Economic activity is indeed but one sector in a great variety of human activities, and like every other sector, it includes the right to freedom, as well as the duty of making responsible use of freedom. But it is important to note that there are specific differences between the trends of modern society and those of the past, even the recent past. Whereas at one time the decisive factor of production was *the land,* and later capital — understood as a total complex of the instruments of production — today the decisive factor is increasingly *the person,* that is, one's knowledge, especially one's scientific knowledge, one's capacity for interrelated and compact organization, as well as one's ability to perceive the needs of others and to satisfy them.

33. However, the risks and problems connected with this kind of process should be pointed out.

The fact is that many people, perhaps the majority today, do not have the means which would enable them to take their place in an effective and humanly dignified way within a productive system in which work is truly central. They have no possibility of acquiring the basic knowledge which would enable them to express their creativity and develop their potential. They have no way of entering the network of knowledge and intercommunication which would enable them to see their qualities appreciated and utilized. Thus, if not actually exploited, they are to a great extent marginalized; economic development takes place over their heads, so to speak, when it does not actually reduce the already narrow scope of their old subsistence economies. They are unable to compete against the goods which are produced in ways which are new and which properly respond to needs, needs which they had previously been accustomed to meeting through traditional forms of organization. Allured by the dazzle of an opulence which is beyond their reach, and at the same time driven by necessity, these people crowd the cities of the Third World where they are often without cultural roots, and where they are exposed to situations of violent uncertainty, without the possibility of becoming integrated. Their dignity is not acknowledged in any real way, and sometimes there are even attempts to eliminate them from history through coercive forms of demographic control which are contrary to human dignity.

Many other people, while not completely marginalized, live

in situations in which the struggle for a bare minimum is uppermost. These are situations in which the rules of the earliest period of capitalism still flourish in conditions of "ruthlessness" in no way inferior to the darkest moments of the first phase of industrialization. In other cases the land is still the central element in the economic process, but those who cultivate it are excluded from ownership and are reduced to a state of quasi-servitude.[71] In these cases, it is still possible today, as in the days of *Rerum Novarum,* to speak of inhuman exploitation. In spite of the great changes which have taken place in the more advanced societies, the human inadequacies of capitalism and the resulting domination of things over people are far from disappearing. In fact, for the poor, to the lack of material goods has been added a lack of knowledge and training which prevents them from escaping their state of humiliating subjection.

Unfortunately, the great majority of people in the Third World still live in such conditions. It would be a mistake, however, to understand this *"world"* in purely geographic terms. In some regions and in some social sectors of that world, development programs have been set up which are centered on the use not so much of the material resources available but of the "human resources."

Even in recent years it was thought that the poorest countries would develop by isolating themselves from the world market and by depending only on their own resources. Recent experience has shown that countries which did this have suffered stagnation and recession, while the countries which experienced development were those which succeeded in taking part in the general interrelated economic activities at the international level. It seems therefore that the chief problem is that of gaining fair access to the international market, based not on the unilateral principle of the exploitation of the natural resources of these countries but on the proper use of human resources.[72]

However, aspects typical of the Third World also appear in

developed countries, where the constant transformation of the methods of production and consumption devalues certain acquired skills and professional expertise, and thus requires a continual effort of retraining and updating. Those who fail to keep up with the times can easily be marginalized, as can the elderly, the young people who are incapable of finding their place in the life of society and, in general, those who are weakest or part of the so-called Fourth World. The situation of women too is far from easy in these conditions.

34. It would appear that, on the level of individual nations and of international relations, *the free market* is the most efficient instrument for utilizing resources and effectively responding to needs. But this is true only for those needs which are "solvent," insofar as they are endowed with purchasing power, and for those resources which are "marketable," insofar as they are capable of obtaining a satisfactory price. But there are many human needs which find no place on the market. It is a strict duty of justice and truth not to allow fundamental human needs to remain unsatisfied, and not to allow those burdened by such needs to perish. It is also necessary to help these needy people to acquire expertise, to enter the circle of exchange, and to develop their skills in order to make the best use of their capacities and resources. Even prior to the logic of a fair exchange of goods and the forms of justice appropriate to it, there exists *something which is due to the person because he is a person,* by reason of his lofty dignity. Inseparable from that required "something" is the possibility to survive and, at the same time, to make an active contribution to the common good of humanity.

In Third World contexts, certain objectives stated by *Rerum Novarum* remain valid, and, in some cases, still constitute a goal yet to be reached, if a person's work and very being are not to be reduced to the level of a mere commodity. These objectives include a sufficient wage for the support of the family, social insurance for old age and unemployment, and adequate protection for the conditions of employment.

35. Here we find a wide range of *opportunities for commitment and effort* in the name of justice on the part of trade unions and other workers' organizations. These defend workers' rights and protect their interests as persons, while fulfilling a vital cultural role, so as to enable workers to participate more fully and honorably in the life of their nation and to assist them along the path of development.

In this sense, it is right to speak of a struggle against an economic system, if the latter is understood as a method of upholding the absolute predominance of capital, the possession of the means of production and of the land, in contrast to the free and personal nature of human work.[73] In the struggle against such a system, what is being proposed as an alternative is not the socialist system, which in fact turns out to be state capitalism, but rather *a society of free work, of enterprise and of participation*. Such a society is not directed against the market, but demands that the market be appropriately controlled by the forces of society and by the State, so as to guarantee that the basic needs of the whole of society are satisfied.

The Church acknowledges the legitimate *role of profit* as an indication that a business is functioning well. When a firm makes a profit, this means that productive factors have been properly employed and corresponding human needs have been duly satisfied. But profitability is not the only indicator of a firm's condition. It is possible for the financial accounts to be in order, and yet for the people — who make up the firm's most valuable asset — to be humiliated and their dignity offended. Besides being morally inadmissible, this will eventually have negative repercussions on the firm's economic efficiency. In fact, the purpose of a business firm is not simply to make a profit, but is to be found in its very existence as a *community of persons* who in various ways are endeavoring to satisfy their basic needs, and who form a particular group at the service of the whole of society. Profit is a regulator of the life of a business, but it is not the only one; *other human and moral factors* must also be considered which, in the long term, are at least equally important for the life of a business.

We have seen that it is unacceptable to say that the defeat of so-called "Real Socialism" leaves capitalism as the only model of economic organization. It is necessary to break down the barriers and monopolies which leave so many countries on the margins of development, and to provide all individuals and nations with the basic conditions which will enable them to share in development. This goal calls for programmed and responsible efforts on the part of the entire international community. Stronger nations must offer weaker ones opportunities for taking their place in international life, and the latter must learn how to use these opportunities by making the necessary efforts and sacrifices and by ensuring political and economic stability, the certainty of better prospects for the future, the improvement of workers' skills, and the training of competent business leaders who are conscious of their responsibilities.[74]

At present, the positive efforts which have been made along these lines are being affected by the still largely unsolved problem of the foreign debt of the poorer countries. The principle that debts must be paid is certainly just. However, it is not right to demand or expect payment when the effect would be the imposition of political choices leading to hunger and despair for entire peoples. It cannot be expected that the debts which have been contracted should be paid at the price of unbearable sacrifices. In such cases it is necessary to find — as in fact is partly happening — ways to lighten, defer or even cancel the debt, compatible with the fundamental right of peoples to subsistence and progress.

36. It would now be helpful to direct our attention to the specific problems and threats emerging within the more advanced

economies and which are related to their particular characteristics. In earlier stages of development, people always lived under the weight of necessity. Their needs were few and were determined, to a degree, by the objective structures of their physical make-up. Economic activity was directed towards satisfying these needs. It is clear that today the problem is not only one of supplying people with a sufficient quantity of goods, but also of responding to a *demand for quality:* the quality of the goods to be produced and consumed, the quality of the services to be enjoyed, the quality of the environment and of life in general.

To call for an existence which is qualitatively more satisfying is of itself legitimate, but one cannot fail to draw attention to the new responsibilities and dangers connected with this phase of history. The manner in which new needs arise and are defined is always marked by a more or less appropriate concept of the human person and of the person's true good. A given culture reveals its overall understanding of life through the choices it makes in production and consumption. It is here that *the phenomenon of consumerism* arises. In singling out new needs and new means to meet them, one must be guided by a comprehensive picture of the person which respects all the dimensions of his being and which subordinates his material and instinctive dimensions to his interior and spiritual ones. If, on the contrary, a direct appeal is made to human instincts — while ignoring in various ways the reality of the person as intelligent and free — then *consumer attitudes and lifestyles* can be created which are objectively improper and often damaging to the person's physical and spiritual health. Of itself, an economic system does not possess criteria for correctly distinguishing new and higher forms of satisfying human needs from artificial new needs which hinder the formation of a mature personality. *Thus a great deal of educational and cultural work* is urgently needed, including the education of consumers in the responsible use of their power of choice, the formation of a strong sense of responsibility among producers and among people in the mass media in particular, as well as the necessary intervention by public authorities.

A striking example of artificial consumption contrary to the health and dignity of the human person, and certainly not easy to control, is the use of drugs. Widespread drug use is a sign of a serious malfunction in the social system; it also implies a materialistic and, in a certain sense, destructive "reading" of human needs. In this way the innovative capacity of a free economy is brought to a one-sided and inadequate conclusion. Drugs, as well as pornography and other forms of consumerism which exploit the frailty of the weak, tend to fill the resulting spiritual void.

It is not wrong to want to live better; what is wrong is a style of life which is presumed to be better when it is directed towards "having" rather than "being," and which wants to have more, not in order to be more but in order to spend life in enjoyment as an end in itself.[75] It is therefore necessary to create lifestyles in which the quest for truth, beauty, goodness and communion with others for the sake of common growth are the factors which determine consumer choices, savings and investments. In this regard, it is not a matter of the duty of charity alone, that is, the duty to give from one's "abundance," and sometimes even out of one's needs, in order to provide what is essential for the life of a poor person. I am referring to the fact that even the decision to invest in one place rather than another, in one productive sector rather than another, is always *a moral and cultural choice.* Given the utter necessity of certain economic conditions and of political stability, the decision to invest, that is, to offer people an opportunity to make good use of their own labor, is also determined by an attitude of human sympathy and trust in Providence, which reveal the human quality of the person making such decisions.

37. Equally worrying is *the ecological question* which accompanies the problem of consumerism and which is closely

connected to it. In their desire to have and to enjoy rather than to be and to grow, people consume the resources of the earth and their own lives in an excessive and disordered way. At the root of the senseless destruction of the natural environment lies an anthropological error, which unfortunately is widespread in our day. Humankind, which discovers its capacity to transform and in a certain sense create the world through its own work, forgets that this is always based on God's prior and original gift of the things that are. People think that they can make arbitrary use of the earth, subjecting it without restraint to their wills, as though the earth did not have its own requisites and a prior God-given purpose, which human beings can indeed develop but must not betray. Instead of carrying out one's role as a cooperator with God in the work of creation, a person sets himself up in place of God and thus ends up provoking a rebellion on the part of nature, which is more tyrannized than governed by him.[76]

In all this, one notes first the poverty or narrowness of the human outlook, motivated as people are by a desire to possess things rather than to relate them to the truth, and lacking that disinterested, unselfish and aesthetic attitude that is born of wonder in the presence of being and of the beauty which enables one to see in visible things the message of the invisible God who created them. In this regard, humanity today must be conscious of its duties and obligations towards future generations.

38. In addition to the irrational destruction of the natural environment, we must also mention the more serious destruction of the *human environment*, something which is by no means receiving the attention it deserves. Although people are rightly worried — though much less than they should be — about preserving the natural habitats of the various animal species threatened with extinction, because they realize that each of these species makes its particular contribution to the balance of nature in general, too little effort is made to *safeguard the moral conditions*

for an authentic "human ecology." Not only has God given the earth to humanity, which must use it with respect for the original good purpose for which it was given, but man too is God's gift to man. A person must therefore respect the natural and moral structure with which he has been endowed. In this context, mention should be made of the serious problems of modern urbanization, of the need for urban planning which is concerned with how people are to live, and of the attention which should be given to a "social ecology" of work.

The human person receives from God its essential dignity and with it the capacity to transcend every social order so as to move towards truth and goodness. But one is also conditioned by the social structure in which one lives, by the education one has received and by the environment. These elements can either help or hinder a person's living in accordance with the truth. The decisions which create a human environment can give rise to specific structures of sin which impede the full realization of those who are in any way oppressed by them. To destroy such structures and replace them with more authentic forms of living in community is a task which demands courage and patience.[77]

39. The first and fundamental structure for "human ecology" is *the family,* in which someone receives his first formative ideas about truth and goodness, and learns what it means to love and to be loved, and thus what it actually means to be a person. Here we mean the *family founded on marriage,* in which the mutual gift of self by husband and wife creates an environment in which children can be born and develop their potentialities, become aware of their dignity and prepare to face their unique and individual destiny. But it often happens that people are discouraged from creating the proper conditions for human reproduction and are led to consider themselves and their lives as a series of sensations to be experienced rather than as a work to be accomplished. The result is a lack of freedom, which causes a person to

reject a commitment to enter into a stable relationship with another person and to bring children into the world, or which leads people to consider children as one of the many "things" which an individual can have or not have, according to taste, and which compete with other possibilities.

It is necessary to go back to seeing the family as the *sanctuary of life*. The family is indeed sacred: it is the place in which life — the gift of God — can be properly welcomed and protected against the many attacks to which it is exposed, and can develop in accordance with what constitutes authentic human growth. In the face of the so-called culture of death, the family is the heart of the culture of life.

Human ingenuity seems to be directed more towards limiting, suppressing or destroying the sources of life — including recourse to abortion, which unfortunately is so widespread in the world — than towards defending and opening up the possibilities of life. The encyclical *Sollicitudo Rei Socialis* denounced systematic anti-childbearing campaigns which, on the basis of a distorted view of the demographic problem and in a climate of "absolute lack of respect for the freedom of choice of the parties involved," often subject them "to intolerable pressures...in order to force them to submit to this new form of oppression."[78] These policies are extending their field of action by the use of new techniques, to the point of poisoning the lives of millions of defenseless human beings, as if in a form of "chemical warfare."

These criticisms are directed not so much against an economic system as against an ethical and cultural system. The economy in fact is only one aspect and one dimension of the whole of human activity. If economic life is absolutized, if the production and consumption of goods become the center of social life and society's only value, not subject to any other value, the reason is to be found not so much in the economic system itself as in the fact that the entire socio-cultural system, by ignoring the ethical and religious dimension, has been weakened, and ends by limiting itself to the production of goods and services alone.[79]

All of this can be summed up by repeating once more that economic freedom is only one element of human freedom. When it becomes autonomous, when man is seen more as a producer or consumer of goods than as a subject who produces and consumes in order to live, then economic freedom loses its necessary relationship to the human person and ends up by alienating and oppressing him.[80]

40. It is the task of the State to provide for the defense and preservation of common goods such as the natural and human environments, which cannot be safeguarded simply by market forces. Just as in the time of primitive capitalism the State had the duty of defending the basic rights of workers, so now, with the new capitalism, the State and all of society have the duty of *defending those collective goods* which, among others, constitute the essential framework for the legitimate pursuit of personal goals on the part of each individual.

Here we find a new limit on the market: there are collective and qualitative needs which cannot be satisfied by market mechanisms. There are important human needs which escape its logic. There are goods which by their very nature cannot and must not be bought or sold. Certainly the mechanisms of the market offer secure advantages: they help to utilize resources better; they promote the exchange of products; above all they give central place to the person's desires and preferences, which, in a contract, meet the desires and preferences of another person. Nevertheless, these mechanisms carry the risk of an "idolatry" of the market, an idolatry which ignores the existence of goods which by their nature are not and cannot be mere commodities.

41. Marxism criticized capitalist bourgeois societies, blaming them for the commercialization and alienation of human existence. This rebuke is of course based on a mistaken and

inadequate idea of alienation, derived solely from the sphere of relationships of production and ownership, that is, giving them a materialistic foundation and moreover denying the legitimacy and positive value of market relationships even in their own sphere. Marxism thus ends up by affirming that only in a collective society can alienation be eliminated. However, the historical experience of socialist countries has sadly demonstrated that collectivism does not do away with alienation but rather increases it, adding to it a lack of basic necessities and economic inefficiency.

The historical experience of the West, for its part, shows that even if the Marxist analysis and its foundation of alienation are false, nevertheless alienation — and the loss of the authentic meaning of life — is a reality in Western societies too. This happens in consumerism, when people are ensnared in a web of false and superficial gratifications rather than being helped to experience their personhood in an authentic and concrete way. Alienation is found also in work, when it is organized so as to ensure maximum returns and profits with no concern whether the worker, through his own labor, grows or diminishes as a person, either through increased sharing in a genuinely supportive community or through increased isolation in a maze of relationships marked by destructive competitiveness and estrangement, in which he is considered only a means and not an end.

The concept of alienation needs to be led back to the Christian vision of reality, by recognizing in alienation a reversal of means and ends. When man does not recognize in himself and in others the value and grandeur of the human person, he effectively deprives himself of the possibility of benefitting from his humanity and of entering into that relationship of solidarity and communion with others for which God created him. Indeed, it is through the free gift of self that one truly finds oneself.[81] This gift is made possible by the human person's essential "capacity for transcendence." One cannot give oneself to a purely human plan for reality, to an abstract ideal or to a false utopia. As a person, one can give oneself to another person or to other persons, and ultimately to God, who is the author of our being and who alone can fully accept our gift.[82] A person is alienated if he refuses to transcend himself and to live the experience of self-giving and of the formation of an authentic human community oriented towards his final destiny, which is God. A society is alienated if its forms of social organization, production and consumption make it more difficult to offer this gift of self and to establish this solidarity between people.

Exploitation, at least in the forms analyzed and described by Karl Marx, has been overcome in Western society. Alienation, however, has not been overcome as it exists in various forms of exploitation, when people use one another, and when they seek an ever more refined satisfaction of their individual and secondary needs, while ignoring the principal and authentic needs which ought to regulate the manner of satisfying the other ones too.[83] A person who is concerned solely or primarily with possessing and enjoying, who is no longer able to control his instincts and passions, or to subordinate them by obedience to the truth, cannot be free: *obedience to the truth* about God and humankind is the first condition of freedom, making it possible for a person to order his needs and desires and to choose the means of satisfying them according to a correct scale of values, so that the ownership of things may become an occasion of personal growth. This growth can be hindered as a result of manipulation by the means of mass communication, which impose fashions and trends of opinion through carefully orchestrated repetition, without it being possible to subject to critical scrutiny the premises on which these fashions and trends are based.

42. Returning now to the initial question: can it perhaps be

said that, after the failure of Communism, capitalism is the victorious social system, and that capitalism should be the goal of the countries now making efforts to rebuild their economy and society? Is this the model which ought to be proposed to the countries of the Third World which are searching for the path to true economic and civil progress?

The answer is obviously complex. If by "capitalism" is meant an economic system which recognizes the fundamental and positive role of buisiness, the market, private property and the resulting responsibility for the means of production, as well as free human creativity in the economic sector, then the answer is certainly in the affirmative, even though it would perhaps be more appropriate to speak of a "business economy," "market economy" or simply "free economy." But if by "capitalism" is meant a system in which freedom in the economic sector is not circumscribed within a strong juridical framework which places it at the service of human freedom in its totality and sees it as a particular aspect of that freedom, the core of which is ethical and religious, then the reply is certainly negative.

The Marxist solution has failed, but the realities of marginalization and exploitation remain in the world, especially the Third World, as does the reality of human alienation, especially in the more advanced countries. Against these phenomena the Church strongly raises her voice. Vast multitudes are still living in conditions of great material and moral poverty. The collapse of the Communist system in so many countries certainly removes an obstacle to facing these problems in an appropriate and realistic way, but it is not enough to bring about their solution. Indeed, there is a risk that a radical capitalistic ideology could spread which refuses even to consider these problems, in the *a priori* belief that any attempt to solve them is doomed to failure, and which blindly entrusts their solution to the free development of market forces.

43. The Church has no models to present; models that are

real and truly effective can only arise within the framework of different historical situations, through the efforts of all those who responsibly confront concrete problems in all their social, economic, political and cultural aspects, as these interact with one another.[84] For such a task the Church offers her social teaching as an *indispensable and ideal orientation,* a teaching which, as already mentioned, recognizes the positive value of the market and of enterprise, but which at the same time points out that these need to be oriented towards the common good. This teaching also recognizes the legitimacy of workers' efforts to obtain full respect for their dignity and to gain broader areas of participation in the life of industrial enterprises so that, while cooperating with others and under the direction of others, they can in a certain sense "work for themselves"[85] through the exercise of their intelligence and freedom.

The integral development of the human person through work does not impede but rather promotes the greater productivity and efficiency of work itself, even though it may weaken consolidated power structures. A business cannot be considered only as a "society of capital goods"; it is also a "society of persons" in which people participate in different ways and with specific responsibilities, whether they supply the necessary capital for the company's activities or take part in such activities through their labor. To achieve these goals there is still need for a broad associated workers' movement, directed towards the liberation and promotion of the whole person.

In the light of today's "new things," we have reread *the relationship between individual or private property and the universal destination of material wealth.* One fulfills oneself by using one's intelligence and freedom. In so doing a person utilizes the things of this world as objects and instruments and makes them his own. The foundation of the right to private initiative and ownership is to be found in this activity. By means of his work a person commits himself, not only for his own sake but also *for others* and *with others*. Each person collaborates in the work of others and for their good. One works in order to provide for the needs of one's family, one's community, one's nation, and ultimately all humanity.[86] Moreover, a person collaborates in the work of his fellow employees, as well as in the work of suppliers and in the customers' use of goods, in a progressively expanding chain of solidarity. Ownership of the means of production, whether in industry or agriculture, is just and legitimate if it serves useful work. It becomes illegitimate, however, when it is not utilized or when it serves to impede the work of others, in an effort to gain a profit which is not the result of the overall expansion of work and the wealth of society, but rather is the result of curbing them or of illicit exploitation, speculation or the breaking of solidarity among working people.[87] Ownership of this kind has no justification, and represents an abuse in the sight of God and humanity.

The obligation to earn one's bread by the sweat of one's brow also presumes the right to do so. A society in which this right is systematically denied, in which economic policies do not allow workers to reach satisfactory levels of employment, cannot be justified from an ethical point of view, nor can that society attain social peace.[88] Just as the person fully realizes himself in the free gift of self, so too ownership morally justifies itself in the creation, at the proper time and in the proper way, of opportunities for work and human growth for all.

Chapter V

State and Culture

44. Pope Leo XIII was aware of the need for a sound *theory of the State* in order to ensure the normal development of the human person's spiritual and temporal activities, both of which are indispensable.[89] For this reason, in one passage of *Rerum Novarum* he presents the organization of society according to the three powers — legislative, executive and judicial — something which at the time represented a novelty in Church teaching.[90] Such an ordering reflects a realistic vision of humankind's social nature, which calls for legislation capable of protecting the freedom of all. To that end, it is preferable that each power be balanced by other powers and by other spheres of responsibility which keep it within proper bounds. This is the principle of the "rule of law," in which the law is sovereign, and not the arbitrary will of individuals.

In modern times, this concept has been opposed by totalitarianism, which, in its Marxist-Leninist form, maintains that some people, by virtue of a deeper knowledge of the laws of the development of society, or through membership of a particular class or through contact with the deeper sources of the collective consciousness, are exempt from error and can therefore arrogate to themselves the exercise of absolute power. It must be added that totalitarianism arises out of a denial of truth in the objective sense.

If there is no transcendent truth, in obedience to which a person achieves his full identity, then there is no sure principle for guaranteeing just relations between people. Their self-interest as a class, group or nation would inevitably set them in opposition to one another. If one does not acknowledge transcendent truth, then the force of power takes over, and each person tends to make full use of the means at his disposal in order to impose his own interests or his own opinion, with no regard for the rights of others. People are then respected only to the extent that they can be exploited for selfish ends. Thus, the root of modern totalitarianism is to be found in the denial of the transcendent dignity of the human person who, as the visible image of the invisible God, is therefore by his very nature the subject of rights which no one may violate — no individual, group, class, nation or State. Not even the majority of a social body may violate these rights, by going against the minority, by isolating, oppressing, or exploiting it, or by attempting to annihilate it.[91]

45. The culture and praxis of totalitarianism also involve a rejection of the Church. The State or the party which claims to be able to lead history towards perfect goodness, and which sets itself above all values, cannot tolerate the affirmation of *an objective criterion of good and evil* beyond the will of those in power, since such a criterion, in given circumstances, could be used to judge their actions. This explains why totalitarianism attempts to destroy the Church, or at least to reduce her to submission, making her an instrument of its own ideological apparatus.[92]

Furthermore, the totalitarian State tends to absorb within itself the nation, society, the family, religious groups and individuals themselves. In defending her own freedom, the Church is also defending the human person, who must obey God rather than men (cf. Acts 5:29), as well as defending the family, the various social organizations and nations — all of which enjoy their own spheres of autonomy and sovereignty.

46. The Church values the democratic system inasmuch as it ensures the participation of citizens in making political choices, guarantees to the governed the possibility both of electing and holding accountable those who govern them, and of replacing them through peaceful means when appropriate.[93] Thus she cannot encourage the formation of narrow ruling groups which usurp the power of the State for individual interests or for ideological ends.

Authentic democracy is possible only in a State ruled by law, and on the basis of a correct conception of the human person. It requires that the necessary conditions be present for the advancement both of the individual through education and formation in true ideals, and of the "subjectivity" of society through the creation of structures of participation and shared responsibility. Nowadays there is a tendency to claim that agnosticism and skeptical relativism are the philosophy and the basic attitude which correspond to democratic forms of political life. Those who are convinced that they know the truth and firmly adhere to it are considered unreliable from a democratic point of view, since they do not accept that truth is determined by the majority, or that it is subject to variation according to different political trends. It must be observed in this regard that if there is no ultimate truth to guide and direct political activity, then ideas and convictions can easily be manipulated for reasons of power. As history demonstrates, a democracy without values easily turns into open or thinly disguised totalitarianism.

Nor does the Church close her eyes to the danger of fanaticism or fundamentalism among those who, in the name of an ideology which purports to be scientific or religious, claim the right to impose on others their own concept of what is true and good. *Christian truth* is not of this kind. Since it is not an ideology, the Christian faith does not presume to imprison changing socio-political realities in a rigid schema, and it recognizes that human life is realized in history in conditions that are diverse and imperfect. Furthermore, in constantly reaffirming the transcendent dignity of the person, the Church's method is always that of respect for freedom.[94]

But freedom attains its full development only by accepting the truth. In a world without truth, freedom loses its foundation and people are exposed to the violence of passion and to manipulation, both open and hidden. The Christian upholds freedom and serves it, constantly offering to others the truth which he has known (cf. Jn 8:31-32), in accordance with the missionary nature of his vocation. While paying heed to every fragment of truth which he encounters in the life experience and in the culture of individuals and of nations, he will not fail to affirm in dialogue with others all that his faith and the correct use of reason have enabled him to understand.[95]

47. Following the collapse of Communist totalitarianism and of many other totalitarian and "national security" regimes, today we are witnessing a predominance, not without signs of opposition, of the democratic ideal, together with lively attention to and concern for human rights. But for this very reason it is necessary for peoples in the process of reforming their systems to give democracy an authentic and solid foundation through the explicit recognition of those rights.[96] Among the most important of these rights, mention must be made of the right to life, an integral part of which is the right of the child to develop in the mother's womb from the moment of conception; the right to live in a united family and in a moral environment conducive to the growth of the child's personality; the right to develop one's intelligence and freedom in seeking and knowing the truth; the right to share in the work which makes wise use of the earth's material resources, and to derive from that work the means to support oneself and one's dependents; and the right freely to establish a family, to have and to rear children through the

responsible exercise of one's sexuality. In a certain sense, the source and synthesis of these rights is religious freedom, understood as the right to live in the truth of one's faith and in conformity with one's transcendent dignity as a person.[97]

Even in countries with democratic forms of government, these rights are not always fully respected. Here we are referring not only to the scandal of abortion, but also to different aspects of a crisis within democracies themselves, which seem at times to have lost the ability to make decisions aimed at the common good. Certain demands which arise within society are sometimes not examined in accordance with criteria of justice and morality, but rather on the basis of the electoral or financial power of the groups promoting them. With time, such distortions of political conduct create distrust and apathy, with a subsequent decline in the political participation and civic spirit of the general population, which feels abused and disillusioned. As a result, there is a growing inability to situate particular interests within the framework of a coherent vision of the common good. The latter is not simply the sum total of particular interests; rather it involves an assessment and integration of those interests on the basis of a balanced hierarchy of values; ultimately, it demands a correct understanding of the dignity and the rights of the person.[98]

The Church respects *the legitimate autonomy of the democratic order* and is not entitled to express preferences for this or that institutional or constitutional solution. Her contribution to the political order is precisely her vision of the dignity of the person revealed in all its fullness in the mystery of the Incarnate Word.[99]

48. These general observations also apply to the *role of the State in the economic sector*. Economic activity, especially the activity of a market economy, cannot be conducted in an institutional, juridical or political vacuum. On the contrary, it presupposes sure guarantees of individual freedom and private property,

as well as a stable currency and efficient public services. Hence the principal task of the State is to guarantee this security, so that those who work and produce can enjoy the fruits of their labors and thus feel encouraged to work efficiently and honestly. The absence of stability, together with the corruption of public officials and the spread of improper sources of growing rich and of easy profits deriving from illegal or purely speculative activities, constitutes one of the chief obstacles to development and to the economic order.

Another task of the State is that of overseeing and directing the exercise of human rights in the economic sector. However, primary responsibility in this area belongs not to the State but to individuals and to the various groups and associations which make up society. The State could not directly ensure the right to work for all its citizens unless it controlled every aspect of economic life and restricted the free initiative of individuals. This does not mean, however, that the State has no competence in this domain, as was claimed by those who argued against any rules in the economic sphere. Rather, the State has a duty to sustain business activities by creating conditions which will ensure job opportunities, by stimulating those activities where they are lacking or by supporting them in moments of crisis.

The State has the further right to intervene when particular monopolies create delays or obstacles to development. In addition to the tasks of harmonizing and guiding development, in exceptional circumstances the State can also exercise a *substitute function,* when social sectors or business systems are too weak or are just getting under way, and are not equal to the task at hand. Such supplementary interventions, which are justified by urgent reasons touching the common good, must be as brief as possible, so as to avoid removing permanently from society and business systems the functions which are properly theirs, and so as to avoid enlarging excessively the sphere of state intervention to the detriment of both economic and civil freedom.

In recent years the range of such intervention has vastly expanded, to the point of creating a new type of state, the so-called "Welfare State." This has happened in some countries in order to respond better to many needs and demands, by remedying forms of poverty and deprivation unworthy of the human person. However, excesses and abuses, especially in recent years, have provoked very harsh criticisms of the Welfare State, dubbed the "Social Assistance State." Malfunctions and defects in the Social Assistance State are the result of an inadequate understanding of the tasks proper to the State. Here again *the principle of subsidiarity* must be respected: a community of a higher order should not interfere in the internal life of a community of a lower order, depriving the latter of its functions, but rather should support it in case of need and help to coordinate its activity with the activities of the rest of society, always with a view to the common good.[100]

By intervening directly and depriving society of its responsibility, the Social Assistance State leads to a loss of human energies and an inordinate increase of public agencies, which are dominated more by bureaucratic ways of thinking than by concern for serving their clients, and which are accompanied by an enormous increase in spending. In fact, it would appear that needs are best understood and satisfied by people who are closest to them and who act as neighbors to those in need. It should be added that certain kinds of demands often call for a response which is not simply material but which is capable of perceiving the deeper human need. One thinks of the condition of refugees, immigrants, the elderly, the sick, and all those in circumstances which call for assistance, such as drug abusers: all these people can be helped effectively only by those who offer them genuine fraternal support, in addition to the necessary care.

49. Faithful to the mission received from Christ her Founder, the Church has always been present and active among the needy, offering them material assistance in ways that neither humiliate

nor reduce them to mere objects of assistance, but which help them to escape their precarious situation by promoting their dignity as persons. With heartfelt gratitude to God it must be pointed out that active charity has never ceased to be practiced in the Church; indeed, today it is showing a manifold and gratifying increase. In this regard, special mention must be made of *volunteer work,* which the Church favors and promotes by urging everyone to cooperate in supporting and encouraging its undertakings.

In order to overcome today's widespread individualistic mentality, what is required is *a concrete commitment to solidarity and charity,* beginning in the family with the mutual support of husband and wife and the care which the different generations give to one another. In this sense the family too can be called a community of work and solidarity. It can happen, however, that when a family does decide to live up fully to its vocation, it finds itself without the necessary support from the State and without sufficient resources. It is urgent therefore to promote not only family policies, but also those social policies which have the family as their principal object, policies which assist the family by providing adequate resources and efficient means of support, both for bringing up children and for looking after the elderly, so as to avoid distancing the latter from the family unit and in order to strengthen relations between generations.[101]

Apart from the family, other intermediate communities exercise primary functions and give life to specific networks of solidarity. These develop as real communities of persons and strengthen the social fabric, preventing society from becoming an anonymous and impersonal mass, as unfortunately often happens today. It is in interrelationships on many levels that a person lives, and that society becomes more "personalized." The individual today is often suffocated between two poles represented by the State and the marketplace. At times it seems as though he exists only as a producer and consumer of goods, or as an object of state administration. People lose sight of the fact that life in society has neither the market nor the State as its final purpose, since life itself has a unique value which the State and the market must serve. Man remains above all a being who seeks the truth and strives to live in that truth, deepening his understanding of it through a dialogue which involves past and future generations.[102]

50. From this open search for truth, which is renewed in every generation, *the culture of a nation* derives its character. Indeed, the heritage of values which has been received and handed down is always challenged by the young. To challenge does not necessarily mean to destroy or reject *a priori,* but above all to put these values to the test in one's own life, and through this existential verification to make them more real, relevant and personal, distinguishing the valid elements in the tradition from false and erroneous ones, or from obsolete forms which can be usefully replaced by others more suited to the times.

In this context, it is appropriate *to recall that evangelization too plays a role in the culture of the various nations,* sustaining culture in its progress towards the truth, and assisting in the work of its purification and enrichment.[103] However, when a culture becomes inward looking, and tries to perpetuate obsolete ways of living by rejecting any exchange or debate with regard to the truth about man, then it becomes sterile and is heading for decadence.

51. All human activity takes place within a culture and interacts with culture. For an adequate formation of a culture, the involvement of the whole person is required, whereby one exercises one's creativity, intelligence, and knowledge of the world and of people. Furthermore, a person displays his capacity for self-control, personal sacrifice, solidarity and readiness to promote the common good. Thus the first and most important task is accomplished within the heart. The way in which one is involved in building one's own future depends on the understanding a

person has of himself and of his own destiny. It is on this level that *the Church's specific and decisive contribution to true culture* is to be found. The Church promotes those aspects of human behavior which favor a true culture of peace, as opposed to models in which the individual is lost in the crowd, in which the role of one's initiative and freedom is neglected, and in which one's greatness is posited in the arts of conflict and war. The Church renders this service to human society *by preaching the truth about the creation of the world,* which God has placed in human hands so that people may make it fruitful and more perfect through their work; and *by preaching the truth about the Redemption,* whereby the Son of God has saved humankind and at the same time has united all people, making them responsible for one another. Sacred Scripture continually speaks to us of an active commitment to our neighbor and demands of us a shared responsibility for all of humanity.

This duty is not limited to one's own family, nation or state, but extends progressively to all humankind, since no one can consider himself extraneous or indifferent to the lot of another member of the human family. No one can say that he is not responsible for the well-being of his brother or sister (cf. Gen 4:9; Lk 10:29-37; Mt 25:31-46). Attentive and pressing concern for one's neighbor in a moment of need — made easier today because of the new means of communication which have brought people closer together — is especially important with regard to the search for ways of resolving international conflicts other than by war. It is not hard to see that the terrifying power of the means of destruction — to which even medium and small-sized countries have access — and the ever closer links between the peoples of the whole world make it very difficult or practically impossible to limit the consequences of a conflict.

52. Pope Benedict XV and his successors clearly understood this danger.[104] I myself, on the occasion of the recent tragic war in

the Persian Gulf, repeated the cry: "War — never again!" No, never again war, which destroys the lives of innocent people, teaches how to kill, throws into upheaval even the lives of those who do the killing and leaves behind a trail of resentment and hatred, thus making it all the more difficult to find a just solution of the very problems which provoked the war. Just as the time has finally come when in individual states a system of private vendetta and reprisal has given way to the rule of law, so too a similar step forward is now urgently needed in the international community. Furthermore, it must not be forgotten that at the root of war there are usually real and serious grievances: injustices suffered, legitimate aspirations frustrated, poverty, and the exploitation of multitudes of desperate people who see no real possibility of improving their lot by peaceful means.

For this reason, another name for peace is *development*.[105] Just as there is a collective responsibility for avoiding war, so too there is a collective responsibility for promoting development. Just as within individual societies it is possible and right to organize a solid economy which will direct the functioning of the market to the common good, so too there is a similar need for adequate interventions on the international level. For this to happen, *a great effort must be made to enhance mutual understanding and knowledge, and to increase the sensitivity of consciences.* This is the culture which is hoped for, one which fosters trust in the human potential of the poor, and consequently in their ability to improve their condition through work or to make a positive contribution to economic prosperity. But to accomplish this, the poor — be they individuals or nations — need to be provided with realistic opportunities. Creating such conditions calls for a *concerted worldwide effort to promote development,* an effort which also involves sacrificing the positions of income and of power enjoyed by the more developed economies.[106]

This may mean making important changes in established

lifestyles, in order to limit the waste of environmental and human resources, thus enabling every individual and all the peoples of the earth to have a sufficient share of those resources. In addition, the new material and spiritual resources must be utilized which are the result of the work and culture of peoples who today are on the margins of the international community, so as to obtain an overall human enrichment of the family of nations.

Chapter VI

The Person Is the Way of the Church

53. Faced with the poverty of the working class, Pope Leo XIII wrote: "We approach this subject with confidence, and in the exercise of the rights which manifestly pertain to us.... By keeping silence we would seem to neglect the duty incumbent on us."[107] During the last hundred years the Church has repeatedly expressed her thinking, while closely following the continuing development of the social question. She has certainly not done this in order to recover former privileges or to impose her own vision. Her sole purpose has been *care and responsibility* for the human person, who has been entrusted to her by Christ himself: for *this person,* whom, as the Second Vatican Council recalls, is the only creature on earth which God willed for its own sake, and for which God has his plan, that is, a share in eternal salvation. We are not dealing here with humanity in the "abstract," but with the real, "concrete," "historical" person. We are dealing with *each individual,* since each one is included in the mystery of Redemption, and through this mystery Christ has united himself with each one forever.[108] It follows that the Church cannot abandon humanity, and that *"this human person* is the primary route that the Church must travel in fulfilling her mission...the way traced out by Christ himself, the way that leads invariably through the mystery of the Incarnation and the Redemption."[109]

This, and this alone, is the principle which inspires the Church's social doctrine. The Church has gradually developed that doctrine in a systematic way, above all in the century that has followed the date we are commemorating, precisely because the horizon of the Church's whole wealth of doctrine is the human being in his concrete reality as sinful and righteous.

54. Today, the Church's social doctrine focuses especially *on the person* as he is involved in a complex network of relationships within modern societies. The human sciences and philosophy are helpful for interpreting *the person's central place within society* and for enabling one to understand oneself better as a "social being." However, a person's true identity is only fully revealed to him through faith, and it is precisely from faith that the Church's social teaching begins. While drawing upon all the contributions made by the sciences and philosophy, her social teaching is aimed at helping everyone on the path of salvation.

The encyclical *Rerum Novarum* can be read as a valid contribution to socio-economic analysis at the end of the nineteenth century, but its specific value derives from the fact that it is a document of the Magisterium and is fully a part of the Church's evangelizing mission, together with many other documents of this nature. Thus the Church's *social teaching* is itself a valid *instrument of evangelization.* As such, it proclaims God and his mystery of salvation in Christ to every human being, and for that very reason reveals man to himself. In this light, and only in this light, does it concern itself with everything else: the human rights of the individual, and in particular of the "working class," the family and education, the duties of the State, the ordering of national and international society, economic life, culture, war and peace, and respect for life from the moment of conception until death.

55. The Church receives "the meaning of the person" from Divine Revelation. "In order to know man, authentic man, man in

his fullness, one must know God," said Pope Paul VI, and he went on to quote Saint Catherine of Siena, who, in prayer, expressed the same idea: "In your nature, O eternal Godhead, I shall know my own nature."[110]

Christian anthropology therefore is really a chapter of theology, and for this reason, the Church's social doctrine, by its concern for the person and by its interest in him and in the way he conducts himself in the world, "belongs to the field...of theology and particularly of moral theology."[111]

The theological dimension is needed both for interpreting and solving present-day problems in human society. It is worth noting that this is true in contrast both to the "atheistic" solution, which deprives humankind of one of its basic dimensions, namely the spiritual one, and to permissive and consumerist solutions, which under various pretexts seek to convince man that he is free from every law and from God himself, thus imprisoning him within a selfishness which ultimately harms both him and others.

When the Church proclaims God's salvation *to humanity,* when she offers and communicates the life of God through the sacraments, when she gives direction to human life through the commandments of love of God and neighbor, she contributes to the enrichment of human dignity. But just as the Church can never abandon her religious and transcendent mission on behalf of humankind, so too she is aware that today her activity meets with particular difficulties and obstacles. That is why she devotes herself with ever new energies and methods to an evangelization which promotes the whole human being. Even on the eve of the third millennium she continues to be "a sign and safeguard of the transcendence of the human person,"[112] as indeed she has always sought to be from the beginning of her existence, walking together with the human race through history. The encyclical *Rerum Novarum* itself is a significant sign of this.

56. On the hundredth anniversary of that encyclical I wish

to thank all those who have devoted themselves to studying, expounding and making better known Christian social teaching. To this end, the cooperation of the local Churches is indispensable, and I would hope that the present anniversary will be a source of fresh enthusiasm for studying, spreading and applying that teaching in various contexts.

In particular, I wish this teaching to be made known and applied in the countries which, following the collapse of "Real Socialism," are experiencing a serious lack of direction in the work of rebuilding. The Western countries, in turn, run the risk of seeing this collapse as a one-sided victory of their own economic system, and thereby failing to make necessary corrections in that system. Meanwhile, the countries of the Third World are experiencing more than ever the tragedy of underdevelopment, which is becoming more serious with each passing day.

After formulating principles and guidelines for the solution of the worker question, Pope Leo XIII made this incisive statement: "Everyone should put his hand to the work which falls to his share, and that at once and straightway, lest the evil which is already so great become through delay absolutely beyond remedy," and he added, "in regard to the Church, her cooperation will never be found lacking."[113]

57. As far as the Church is concerned, the social message of the Gospel must not be considered a theory, but above all else a basis and a motivation for action. Inspired by this message, some of the first Christians distributed their goods to the poor, bearing witness to the fact that, despite different social origins, it was possible for people to live together in peace and harmony. Through the power of the Gospel, down the centuries monks tilled the land, men and women religious founded hospitals and shelters for the poor, confraternities as well as individual men and women of all states of life devoted themselves to the needy and to those on the margins of society, convinced as they were that Christ's

words "as you did it to one of the least of these my brethren, you did it to me" (Mt 25:40) were not intended to remain a pious wish, but were meant to become a concrete life commitment.

Today more than ever, the Church is aware that her social message will gain credibility more immediately from the *witness of actions* than as a result of its internal logic and consistency. This awareness is also a source of her preferential option for the poor, which is never exclusive or discriminatory towards other groups. This option is not limited to material poverty, since it is well known that there are many other forms of poverty, especially in modern society — not only economic but cultural and spiritual poverty as well. The Church's love for the poor, which is essential for her and a part of her constant tradition, impels her to give attention to a world in which poverty is threatening to assume massive proportions in spite of technological and economic progress. In the countries of the West, different forms of poverty are being experienced by groups which live on the margins of society, by the elderly and the sick, by the victims of consumerism, and even more immediately by so many refugees and migrants. In the developing countries, tragic crises loom on the horizon unless internationally coordinated measures are taken before it is too late.

58. Love for others, and in the first place love for the poor, in whom the Church sees Christ himself, is made concrete in the *promotion of justice.* Justice will never be fully attained unless people see in the poor person, who is asking for help in order to survive, not an annoyance or a burden, but an opportunity for showing kindness and a chance for greater enrichment. Only such an awareness can give the courage needed to face the risk and the change involved in every authentic attempt to come to the aid of another. It is not merely a matter of "giving from one's surplus," but of helping entire peoples which are presently excluded or marginalized to enter into the sphere of economic and human

development. For this to happen, it is not enough to draw on the surplus goods which in fact our world abundantly produces; it requires above all a change of lifestyles, of models of production and consumption, and of the established structures of power which today govern societies. Nor is it a matter of eliminating instruments of social organization which have proved useful, but rather of orienting them according to an adequate notion of the common good in relation to the whole human family. Today we are facing the so-called "globalization" of the economy, a phenomenon which is not to be dismissed, since it can create unusual opportunities for greater prosperity. There is a growing feeling, however, that this increasing internationalization of the economy ought to be accompanied by effective international agencies which will oversee and direct the economy to the common good, something that an individual state, even if it were the most powerful on earth, would not be in a position to do. In order to achieve this result, it is necessary that there be increased coordination among the more powerful countries, and that in international agencies the interests of the whole human family be equally represented. It is also necessary that in evaluating the consequences of their decisions, these agencies always give sufficient consideration to peoples and countries which have little weight in the international market, but which are burdened by the most acute and desperate needs, and are thus more dependent on support for their development. Much remains to be done in this area.

59. Therefore, in order that the demands of justice may be met, and attempts to achieve this goal may succeed, what is needed is *the gift of grace, a gift* which comes from God. Grace, in cooperation with human freedom, constitutes that mysterious presence of God in history which is Providence.

The newness which is experienced in following Christ demands to be communicated to other people in their concrete difficulties, struggles, problems and challenges, so that these can then be illuminated and made more human in the light of faith. Faith not only helps people to find solutions; it makes even situations of suffering humanly bearable, so that in these situations people will not become lost or forget their dignity and vocation.

In addition, the Church's social teaching has an important interdisciplinary dimension. In order better to incarnate the one truth about man in different and constantly changing social, economic and political contexts, this teaching enters into dialogue with the various disciplines concerned with humankind. It assimilates what these disciplines have to contribute, and helps them to open themselves to a broader horizon, aimed at serving the individual person who is acknowledged and loved in the fullness of his or her vocation.

Parallel with the interdisciplinary aspect, mention should also be made of the practical and as it were experiential dimension of this teaching, which is to be found at the crossroads where Christian life and conscience come into contact with the real world. This teaching is seen in the efforts of individuals, families, people involved in cultural and social life, as well as politicians and statesmen to give it a concrete form and application in history.

60. In proclaiming the principles for a solution of the worker question, Pope Leo XIII wrote: "This most serious question demands the attention and the efforts of others."[114] He was convinced that the grave problems caused by industrial society could be solved only by cooperation between all forces. This affirmation has become a permanent element of the Church's social teaching, and also explains why Pope John XXIII addressed his encyclical on peace to "all people of good will."

Pope Leo, however, acknowledged with sorrow that the ideologies of his time, especially Liberalism and Marxism, rejected such cooperation. Since then, many things have changed, especially in recent years. The world today is ever more aware that solving serious national and international problems is not just a matter of economic production or of juridical or social organization, but also calls for specific ethical and religious values, as well as changes of mentality, behavior and structures. The Church feels a particular responsibility to offer this contribution and, as I have written in the encyclical *Sollicitudo Rei Socialis,* there is a reasonable hope that the many people who profess no religion will also contribute to providing the social question with the necessary ethical foundation.[115]

In that same encyclical I also addressed an appeal to the Christian Churches and to all the great world religions, inviting them to offer the unanimous witness of our common convictions regarding the dignity of the human person, created by God.[116] In fact I am convinced that the various religions, now and in the future, will have a preeminent role in preserving peace and in building a society worthy of humanity.

Indeed, openness to dialogue and to cooperation is required of all people of good will, and in particular of individuals and groups with specific responsibilities in the areas of politics, economics and social life, at both the national and international levels.

61. At the beginning of industrialized society, it was "a yoke little better than that of slavery itself" which led my predecessor to speak out *in defense of the human person.* Over the past hundred years the Church has remained faithful to this duty. Indeed, she intervened in the turbulent period of class struggle after the First World War in order to defend people from economic exploitation and from the tyranny of the totalitarian systems. After the Second World War, she put the dignity of the person at the center of her social messages, insisting that material goods were meant for all, and that the social order ought to be free of oppression and based on a spirit of cooperation and solidarity. The Church has con-

stantly repeated that the person and society need not only material goods but spiritual and religious values as well. Furthermore, as she has become more aware of the fact that too many people live, not in the prosperity of the Western world, but in the poverty of the developing countries amid conditions which are still "a yoke little better than that of slavery itself," she has felt and continues to feel obliged to denounce this fact with absolute clarity and frankness, although she knows that her call will not always win favor with everyone.

One hundred years after the publication of *Rerum Novarum,* the Church finds herself still facing "new things" and new challenges. The centenary celebration should therefore confirm the commitment of all people of good will and of believers in particular.

62. The present encyclical has looked at the past, but above all it is directed to the future. Like *Rerum Novarum,* it comes almost at the threshold of a new century, and its intention, with God's help, is to prepare for that moment.

In every age the true and perennial "newness of things" comes from the infinite power of God, who says: "Behold, I make all things new" (Rev 21:5). These words refer to the fulfillment of history, when Christ "delivers the Kingdom to God the Father...that God may be everything to everyone" (1 Cor 15:24, 28). But the Christian well knows that the newness which we await in its fullness at the Lord's second coming has been present since the creation of the world, and in a special way since the time when God became man in Jesus Christ and brought about a "new creation" with him and through him (2 Cor 5:17; Gal 6:15).

In concluding this encyclical I again give thanks to Almighty God, who has granted his Church the light and strength to accompany humanity on its earthly journey towards its eternal destiny. In the third millennium too, the Church will be faithful *in making humanity's way her own,* knowing that she does not walk alone, but with Christ her Lord. It is Christ who made man's way his own, and who guides him, even when he is unaware of it.

Mary, the Mother of the Redeemer, constantly remained beside Christ in his journey towards the human family and in its midst, and she goes before the Church on the pilgrimage of faith. May her maternal intercession accompany humanity towards the next millennium, in fidelity to him who "is the same yesterday and today and for ever" (cf. Heb 13:8), Jesus Christ our Lord, in whose name I cordially impart my blessing to all.

Given in Rome, at Saint Peter's, on May 1, the Memorial of Saint Joseph the Worker, in the year 1991, the thirteenth of my pontificate.

Joannes Paulus PP. II

Notes

1. Leo XIII, Encyclical Letter *Rerum Novarum* (May 15, 1891): *Leonis XIII P.M. Acta*, XI, Romae 1892, 97-144.

2. Pius XI, Encyclical Letter *Quadragesimo Anno* (May 15, 1931): *AAS* 23 (1931), 177-228; Pius XII, Radio Message of June 1, 1941: *AAS* 33 (1941), 195-205; John XXIII, Encyclical Letter *Mater et Magistra* (May 15, 1961): *AAS* 53 (1961), 401-464; Paul VI, Apostolic Epistle *Octogesima Adveniens* (May 14, 1971): *AAS* 63 (1971), 401-441.

3. Cf. Pius XI, Encyclical Letter *Quadragesimo Anno*, III, *loc. cit.*, 228.

4. Encyclical Letter *Laborem Exercens* (September 14, 1981): *AAS* 73 (1981), 577-647; Encyclical Letter *Sollicitudo Rei Socialis* (December 30, 1987): *AAS* 80 (1988), 513-586.

5. Cf. St. Irenaeus, *Adversus Haereses*, I, 10, 1; III, 4, 1: *PG* 7, 549f.; 855f.; *S. Ch.* 264, 154f.; 211, 44-46.

6. Leo XIII, Encyclical Letter *Rerum Novarum: loc. cit.*, 132.

7. Cf., e.g., Leo XIII, Encyclical Epistle *Arcanum Divinae Sapientiae* (February 10, 1880): *Leonis XIII P.M. Acta*, II, Romae 1882, 10-40; Encyclical Epistle *Diuturnum Illud* (June 29, 1881): *Leonis XIII P.M. Acta*, II, Romae 1882, 269-287; Encyclical Letter *Libertas Praestantissimum* (June 20, 1888): *Leonis XIII P.M. Acta*, VIII, Romae 1889, 212-246; Encyclical Epistle *Graves de communi* (January 18, 1901): *Leonis XIII P.M. Acta, XXI*, Romae 1902, 3-20.

8. Encyclical Letter *Rerum Novarum: loc. cit.*, 97.

9. *Ibid.: loc. cit.*, 98.

10. Cf. *ibid.: loc. cit.*, 109f.

11. Cf. *ibid.:* description of working conditions; 44: anti-Christian workers' associations: *loc. cit.*, 110f.; 136f.

12. *Ibid.: loc. cit.*, 130; cf. also 114f.

13. *Ibid.: loc. cit.*, 130.

14. *Ibid.: loc. cit.*, 123.

15. Cf. Encyclical Letter *Laborem Exercens*, 1, 2, 6: *loc. cit.*, 578-583; 589-592.

16. Cf. Encyclical Letter *Rerum Novarum: loc. cit.,* 99-107.

17. Cf. *ibid.: loc. cit.,* 102f.

18. Cf. *ibid.: loc. cit.,* 101-104.

19. Cf. *ibid.: loc. cit.,* 134f.; 137f.

20. *Ibid.: loc. cit.,* 135.

21. Cf. *Ibid.: loc. cit.,* 128-129.

22. *Ibid.: loc. cit.,* 129.

23. *Ibid.: loc. cit.,* 129.

24. *Ibid.: loc. cit.,* 130f.

25. *Ibid.: loc. cit.,* 131.

26. Cf. Universal Declaration of Human Rights.

27. Cf. Encyclical Letter *Rerum Novarum: loc. cit.,* 121-123.

28. Cf. *ibid.: loc. cit.,* 127.

29. *Ibid.: loc. cit.,* 126f.

30. Cf Universal Declaration of Human Rights; Declaration on the elimination of every form of intolerance and discrimination based on religion or convictions.

31. Second Vatican Ecumenical Council, Declaration on Religious Freedom *Dignitatis Humanae;* John Paul II, Letter to Heads of State (September 1, 1980): *AAS* 72 (1980), 1252-1260; Message for the 1988 World Day of Peace (January 1, 1988): *AAS* 80 (1988), 278-286.

32. Cf. Encyclical Letter *Rerum Novarum:* 42: *loc. cit.,* 99-105; 130f.; 135.

33. *Ibid.: loc. cit.,* 125.

34. Cf. Encyclical Letter *Sollicitudo Rei Socialis,* 38-40: *loc. cit.,* 564-569; cf. also John XXIII, Encyclical Letter *Mater et Magistra, loc. cit.,* 407.

35. Cf. Leo XIII, Encyclical Letter *Rerum Novarum: loc. cit.,* 114-116; Pius XI, Encyclical Letter *Quadragesimo Anno,* III, *loc. cit.,* 208; Paul VI, Homily for the Closing of the Holy Year (December 25, 1975): *AAS* 68 (1976), 145; Message for the 1977 World Day of Peace (January 1, 1977): *AAS* 68 (1976), 709.

36. Encyclical Letter *Sollicitudo Rei Socialis,* 42: *loc. cit.,* 572.

37. Cf. Encyclical Letter *Rerum Novarum: loc. cit.,* 101f.; 104f.; 130f.; 136.

38. Second Vatican Ecumenical Council, Pastoral Constitution on the Church in the World of Today *Gaudium et Spes,* 24.

39. Encyclical Letter *Rerum Novarum: loc. cit.,* 99.

40. Cf. Encyclical Letter *Sollicitudo Rei Socialis,* 15, 28: *loc. cit.,* 530; 548ff.

41. Cf. Encyclical Letter *Laborem Exercens,* 11-15: *loc. cit.,* 602-618.

42. Pius XI, Encyclical Letter *Quadragesimo Anno,* III, 113: *loc. cit.,* 213.

43. Cf. Encyclical Letter *Rerum Novarum: loc. cit.,* 121-125.

44. Cf. Encyclical Letter *Laborem Exercens,* 20: *loc. cit.,* 629-632; Discourse to the International Labor Organization (I.L.O.) in Geneva (June 15, 1982): *Insegnamenti* V/2 (1982), 2250-2266; Paul VI, Discourse to the same Organization (June 10, 1969): *AAS* 61 (1969), 491-502.

45. Cf. Encyclical Letter *Laborem Exercens,* 8: *loc. cit.,* 594-598.

46. Cf. Pius XI, Encyclical Letter *Quadragesimo Anno,* 14: *loc. cit.,* 178-181.

47. Cf. Encyclical Epistle *Arcanum Divinae Sapientiae* (February 10, 1880): *Leonis XIII P.M. Acta,* II, Romae 1882, 10-40; Encyclical Epistle *Diuturnum Illud* (June 29, 1881): *Leonis XIII P.M. Acta,* II, Romae 1882, 269-287; Encyclical Epistle *Immortale Dei* (November 1, 1885): *Leonis XIII P.M. Acta,* V, Romae 1886, 118-150; Encyclical Letter *Sapientiae Christianae* (January 10, 1890): *Leonis XIII P.M. Acta,* X, Romae 1891, 10-41; Encyclical Epistle *Quod Apostolici Muneris* (December 28, 1878): *Leonis XIII P.M. Acta,* I, Romae 1881, 170-183; Encyclical Letter *Libertas Praestantissimum* (June 20, 1888): *Leonis XIII P.M. Acta,* VIII, Romae 1889, 212-246.

48. Cf. Leo XIII, Encyclical Letter *Libertas Praestantissimum,* 10: *loc. cit.,* 224-226.

49. Cf. Message for the 1980 World Day of Peace: *AAS* 71 (1979), 1572-1580.

50. Cf. Encyclical Letter *Sollicitudo Rei Socialis,* 20: *loc. cit.,* 536f.

51. Cf. John XXIII, Encyclical Letter *Pacem in Terris* (April 11, 1963), III: *AAS* 55 (1963), 286-289.

52. Cf. Universal Declaration of Human Rights, issued in 1948; John XXIII, Encyclical Letter *Pacem in Terris,* IV: *loc. cit.,* 291-296; "Final Act" of the Conference on Cooperation and Security in Europe, Helsinki, 1975.

53. Cf. Paul VI, Encyclical Letter *Populorum Progressio* (March 26, 1967), 61-65: *AAS* 59 (1967), 287-289.

54. Cf. Message for the 1980 World Day of Peace: *loc. cit.,* 1572-1580.

55. Cf. Second Vatican Ecumenical Council, Pastoral Constitution on the Church in the World of Today *Gaudium et Spes,* 36; 39.

56. Cf. Apostolic Exhortation *Christifideles Laici* (December 30, 1988), 32-44: *AAS* 81 (1989), 431-481.

57. Cf. Encyclical Letter *Laborem Exercens,* 20: *loc. cit.,* 629-632.

58. Cf Congregation for the Doctrine of the Faith, Instruction on Christian Freedom and Liberation *Libertatis Conscientia* (March 22, 1986):

AAS 79 (1987), 554-599.

59. Cf. Discourse at the Headquarters of the E.C.W.A. on the occasion of the Tenth Anniversary of the "Appeal for the Sahel" (Ouagadougou, Burkina Faso, January 29, 1990): *AAS* 82 (1990), 816-821.

60. Cf. John XXIII, Encyclical Letter *Pacem in Terris,* III: *loc. cit.,* 286-288.

61. Cf. Encyclical Letter *Sollicitudo Rei Socialis,* 27-28: *loc. cit.,* 547-550; Paul VI, Encyclical Letter *Populorum Progressio,* 43-44: *loc. cit.,* 278f.

62. Cf. Encyclical Letter *Sollicitudo Rei Socialis,* 29-31: *loc. cit.,* 550-556.

63. Cf. Helsinki Final Act and Vienna Accord; Leo XIII, Encyclical Letter *Libertas Praestantissimum,* 5: *loc. cit.,* 215-217.

64. Cf. Encyclical Letter *Redemptoris Missio* (December 7, 1990), 7: *L'Osservatore Romano,* January 23, 1991.

65. Cf. Encyclical Letter *Rerum Novarum: loc. cit.,* 99-107; 131-133.

66. *Ibid.,* 111-113f.

67. Cf. Pius XI, Encyclical Letter *Quadragesimo Anno,* II; *loc. cit.,* 191; Pius XII, Radio Message on June 1, 1941: *loc. cit.,* 199; John XXIII, Encyclical Letter *Mater et Magistra: loc. cit.,* 428-429; Paul VI, Encyclical Letter *Populorum Progressio,* 22-24: *loc. cit.,* 268f.

68. Second Vatican Ecumenical Council, Pastoral Constitution on the Church in the World of Today *Gaudium et Spes,* 69; 71.

69. Cf. Discourse to Latin American Bishops at Puebla (January 28, 1979), III, 4: *AAS* 71 (1979), 199-201; Encyclical Letter *Laborem Exercens,* 14: *loc. cit.,* 612-616; Encyclical Letter *Sollicitudo Rei Socialis,* 42: *loc. cit.,* 572-574.

70. Cf. Encyclical Letter *Sollicitudo Rei Socialis,* 15: *loc. cit.,* 528-531.

71. Cf. Encyclical Letter *Laborem Exercens,* 21: *loc. cit.,* 632-634.

72. Cf. Paul VI, Encyclical Letter *Populorum Progressio,* 33-42: *loc. cit.,* 273-278.

73. Cf. Encyclical Letter *Laborem Exercens,* 7: *loc. cit.,* 592-594.

74. Cf. *ibid.,* 8: *loc. cit.,* 594-598.

75. Cf. Second Vatican Ecumenical Council, Pastoral Constitution on the Church in the World of Today *Gaudium et Spes,* 35; Paul VI, Encyclical Letter *Populorum Progressio,* 19: *loc. cit.,* 266f.

76. Cf. Encyclical Letter *Sollicitudo Rei Socialis,* 34: *loc. cit.,* 559f.; Message for the 1990 World Day of Peace: *AAS* 82 (1990), 147-156.

77. Cf. Apostolic Exhortation *Reconciliatio et Poenitentia* (December 2, 1984), 16: *AAS* 77 (1985), 213-217; Pius XI, Encyclical Letter *Quadragesimo Anno,* III: *loc. cit.,* 219.

78. Encyclical Letter *Sollicitudo Rei Socialis*, 25: *loc. cit.*, 544.

79. Cf. *ibid.*, 34: *loc. cit.*, 559f.

80. Cf. Encyclical Letter *Redemptor Hominis* (March 4, 1979), 15: *AAS* 71 (1979), 286-289.

81. Cf. Second Vatican Ecumenical Council, Pastoral Constitution on the Church in the World of Today *Gaudium et Spes*, 24.

82. Cf. *ibid.*, 41.

83. Cf. *ibid.*, 26.

84. Cf. Second Vatican Ecumenical Council, Pastoral Constitution on the Church in the World of Today *Gaudium et Spes*, 36; Paul VI, Apostolic Epistle *Octogesima Adveniens*, 2-5: *loc. cit.*, 402-405.

85. Cf. Encyclical Letter *Laborem Exercens*, 15: *loc. cit.*, 616-618.

86. Cf. *ibid.*, 10: *loc. cit.*, 600-602.

87. *Ibid.*, 14: *loc. cit.*, 612-616.

88. Cf. *ibid.*, 18: *loc. cit.*, 622-625.

89. Cf. Encyclical Letter *Rerum Novarum: loc. cit.*, 126-128.

90. *Ibid.*, 121f.

91. Cf. Leo XIII, Encyclical Letter *Libertas Praestantissimum: loc. cit.*, 224-226.

92. Cf. Second Vatican Ecumenical Council, Pastoral Constitution on the Church in the World of Today *Gaudium et Spes*, 76.

93. Cf. *ibid.*, 29; Pius XII, Christmas Radio Message on December 24, 1944: *AAS* 37 (1945), 10-20.

94. Cf. Second Vatican Ecumenical Council, Declaration on Religious Freedom *Dignitatis Humanae*.

95. Cf. Encyclical Letter *Redemptoris Missio*, 11: *L'Osservatore Romano*, January 23, 1991.

96. Cf. Encyclical Letter *Redemptor Hominis*, 17: *loc. cit.*, 270-272.

97. Cf. *Message for the 1988 World Day of Peace: loc. cit.*, 1572-1580; *Message for the 1991 World Day of Peace: L'Osservatore Romano*, December 19, 1990; Second Vatican Ecumenical Council, Declaration on Religious Freedom *Dignitatis Humanae*, 1-2.

98. Second Vatican Ecumenical Council, Pastoral Constitution on the Church in the World of Today *Gaudium et Spes*, 26.

99. Cf. *ibid.*, 22.

100. Pius XI, Encyclical Letter *Quadragesimo Anno*, I : *loc. cit.*, 184-186.

101. Cf. Apostolic Exhortation *Familiaris Consortio* (November 22, 1981), 45: *AAS* 74 (1982), 136f.

102. Cf. Discourse to UNESCO (June 2, 1980): *AAS* 72 (1980), 735-752.

103. Cf. Encyclical Letter *Redemptoris Missio,* 39; 52 *L'Osservatore Romano,* January 23, 1991.

104. Cf. Benedict XV, Exhortation *Ubi Primum* (September 8, 1914): *AAS* 6 (1914), 501f.; Pius XI, Radio Message to the Catholic Faithful and to the entire world (September 29, 1938): *AAS* 30 (1938), 309f.; Pius XII, Radio Message to the entire world (August 24, 1939): *AAS* 31 (1939), 333-335; John XXIII, Encyclical Letter *Pacem in Terris,* III: *loc. cit.,* 285-289; Paul VI, Discourse at the United Nations (October 4, 1965): *AAS* 57 (1965), 877-885.

105. Cf. Paul VI, Encyclical Letter *Populorum Progressio,* 76-77: *loc. cit.,* 294f.

106. Cf. Apostolic Exhortation *Familiaris Consortio,* 48: *loc. cit.,* 139f.

107. Encyclical Letter *Rerum Novarum: loc. cit.,* 107.

108. Cf. Encyclical Letter *Redemptor Hominis,* 13: *loc. cit.,* 283.

109. *Ibid.,* 14: *loc. cit.,* 284f.

110. Paul VI, Homily at the Final Public Session of the Second Vatican Ecumenical Council (December 7, 1965): *AAS* 58 (1966), 58.

111. Encyclical Letter *Sollicitudo Rei Socialis,* 41: *loc. cit.,* 571.

112. Second Vatican Ecumenical Council, Pastoral Constitution on the Church in the World of Today *Gaudium et Spes,* 76; cf. John Paul II, Encyclical Letter *Redemptor Hominis,* 13: *loc. cit.,* 283.

113. Encyclical Letter *Rerum Novarum: loc. cit.,* 143.

114. *Ibid.,* 107.

115. Cf. Encyclical Letter *Sollicitudo Rei Socialis,* 38: *loc. cit.,* 564-566.

116. *Ibid.,* 47: *loc. cit.,* 582.

SP St. Paul Book & Media Centers:

Alexandria, VA
Anchorage, AK
Boston, MA
Charleston, SC
Chicago, IL
Cleveland, OH
Dedham, MA
Edison, NJ
Honolulu, HI
Los Angeles, CA
Miami, FL
New Orleans, LA
New York, NY
King of Prussia, PA
San Antonio, TX
San Diego, CA
San Francisco, CA
St. Louis, MO
Staten Island, NY
Toronto, Ontario, CANADA